Vegetarian Delights

A HEARTY COLLECTION OF NATURAL FOOD RECIPES

BY BARBARA E. ECHOLS

Woodbury, New York • London • Toronto • Sydney

All inquiries should be addressed to:

Barron's Educational Series, Inc.
113 Crossways Park Drive
Woodbury, New York 11797

Library of Congress Catalog Card No. 80-16610

Cloth Edition
International Standard Book No. 0-8120-5433-4

Library of Congress Cataloging in Publication Data

Echols, Barbara E
    Vegetarian Delights

    Bibliography: p. 316
    Includes index.
    1. Vegetarian cookery.   I. Title.
TX837.E33   641.5′636   80-16610
ISBN 0-8120-5433-4

Credits:
Photography:

  Matthew Klein, color photographs
  Andrea Swenson, food stylist
  Wonsook Kim, stylist

Jacket and cover design: Milton Glaser, Inc.

Book design: Milton Glaser, Inc.

PRINTED IN THE UNITED STATES OF AMERICA

2345   049   9876543

CONTENTS

Preface   *5*

1. Vegetarianism: Facts and Fancy   *9*
2. A Trip to Your Local Natural Foods Store   *17*
3. Food Additives and Pesticides   *33*

Recipes   *43*

4. The Basics — Only Better!   *45*
   - Spice Mixtures ———— *46*
   - Flavored Butters ———— *52*
   - Low-Fat Substitutes —— *55*
   - Vinegars ———— *59*
   - Marinades ———— *62*
   - Salad Dressings ———— *65*
   - Sauces ———— *68*
   - Stocks ———— *75*

5. Rice and Other Tasty Grains   *77*
   - Rice ———— *78*
   - Barley, Bulgur, and Buckwheat ———— *89*
   - Corn (Grits) ———— *99*
   - Some Other Items —— *101*

6. Vegetables — The Wonders of the Garden   *105*
   - Asparagus ———— *106*
   - Beets ———— *110*
   - Broccoli ———— *112*
   - Cabbage ———— *115*
   - Carrots ———— *117*
   - Celery ———— *118*
   - Eggplant ———— *119*
   - Green Beans ———— *122*
   - Lima Beans ———— *124*
   - Mushrooms ———— *125*
   - Onions ———— *132*
   - Peas ———— *135*
   - Peppers ———— *136*
   - Potatoes ———— *137*
   - Spinach ———— *139*
   - Tomatoes ———— *149*
   - Zucchini ———— *151*
   - Mixed Vegetables —— *155*

7. Dried Beans for All Occasions   *159*

8. Bean Sprouts and Soybean Products   *183*
Bean Sprouts ———— *184*   Tempeh ————— *191*
Miso ————————— *190*   Tofu ——————— *192*

9. Eggs, Cheese, and Pasta   *195*

10. Yogurt and Yogurt Dishes   *213*

11. Fish, for the Part-Time Vegetarian   *221*

12. Desserts — The Finishing Touches   *245*
Fruit Dishes ———————————— *246*
Frozen Desserts ————————— *253*
A Sweet Miscellany ———————— *255*

13. Sandwiches for Midday Meals   *259*

14. Snacks and Special Treat   *269*
Nuts and Chips ——————————— *270*
Sweet Treats ———————————— *278*
Beverage Snacks ————————— *283*

15. Bread, Biscuits, and Other Baked Goods   *289*
Yeast Breads ———— *291*   Sweet Breads ———— *308*
Biscuits ——————— *298*   Cookies ——————— *310*
Muffins ——————— *301*

Recommended Reading   *316*

Index   *317*

PREFACE

In 1973, as I was gathering material for my book *The Commonsense Guide to Good Eating*,* I became very interested in the vegetarian life-style. My research indicated that the vegetarians included in a study done by scientists had a markedly lower incidence of heart disease than did nonvegetarians. Additionally vegetarians were much trimmer than the general population. Could I become a vegetarian, I asked myself? No! was the resounding answer. A life of carrots and peas definitely was not for me.

In 1974 I contacted a group of students at the Carolina Friends School. I was interested in the extent of their knowledge about the relationship of nutrition to health in general, and about their perceived needs in specific. Fortunately for me, a number of the students were practicing vegetarians of long standing, and they introduced me to the wonderful world of vegetarian cooking.

The road from carrots and peas to vegetarian nut roast was not without its obstacles, however. I never had cooked a dried bean, never had even heard of many of the products that were discussed, and hardly could find whole-wheat flour in the supermarket. Today I not only know mung-bean sprouts when I see them, but I actually grow them in my own

---

*Echols, B. and Arena, J. *The Commonsense Guide to Good Eating.* Barron's Educational Series, Inc., Woodbury, New York, 1978.

kitchen. I recognize most of those here-to-fore mysterious ingredients, know which ones I like and which I dislike, and buy many of them locally. In other words, I have come a long, long way.

I am still impressed by the potential health benefits of a diet that is relatively high in fiber and low in saturated fats — in other words, a vegetarian diet. Additionally I have discovered delicious and economical foods that I never knew existed. Meat and poultry still find their way to my table, but much less frequently than before. Certainly my menus are more varied and exciting than in the old meat-and-potatoes days.

Remembering my own painful odyssey through the land of vegetarian cookbooks and natural foods stores, I have included all the information that you — a beginner — will need. Up until now, most vegetarian cookbooks were written for very dedicated people, and they waxed eloquently about the virtues of a totally meatless diet. But many people come to vegetarianism in other than political ways. Some are attracted, as I was, by the healthful benefits; others find that preparing meatless dishes can be less costly without sacrificing nutrition; still others are intrigued by the different ingredients that show up in vegetarian cooking. And many, many people want to include more vegetable dishes in their menus, but don't really want to go all the way. I've attempted to prove that everyone can reap the benefits of vegetarian life, even without becoming total vegetarians.

This is strictly a book for beginners. If you have wanted to try some of those newer ingredients appearing on the shelves of your supermarket, or if you are always tempted by the strange items in the natural foods store around the corner, then you will find the means for doing this in the pages that follow. I describe each major ingredient of vegetarian gourmet: its physical appearance, storage requirements, general and specific cooking instructions, flavor characteristics, and serving suggestions. The recipes are simple to prepare and use ingredients that are fairly common. The dishes are tasty and, for many readers, may be quite a change from what they are used to; but this collection is not a gourmet cookbook. Rather, you will find that this book is a how-to-do-it and a why-to-do-it manual. It contains nutritional information, shopping tips, menu-planning suggestions, and other bits of miscellanea. This is "my" cookbook; I hope that it will soon be the beginning of yours as well.

CHAPTER 1

Vegetarianism:
Facts and Fancy

VEGETARIANISM: FACTS AND FANCY

There are many degrees of vegetarianism, ranging from lacto-ovo-vegetarians who use eggs and dairy products such as milk, cheese, and butter but who exclude meat, to mono-vegetarians who eat only one food, such as brown rice. There are also many reasons for these dietary preferences.

Vegetarianism is not new. It has long been popular in the Far East, where there is a belief in reincarnation and where cattle are precious and refrigerators are scarce. In the United States, many people avoid meat for a variety of reasons, and they are, or probably will be, rearing their children in like fashion. Many vegetarians hold that life in all forms is sacred, and that all creatures have the right to live out their normal life span. Others maintain that animal meats are not healthy because they are being injected with too many hormones and antibiotics. Still others say that it takes more land to raise livestock and their feed than it does to raise grain for humans; hence eating meat is a wasteful use of our limited space. Then, too, some groups adhere to a vegetarian diet because of the high cost of meat or as part of their religious or spiritual life.

Science can suggest yet another reason. Many studies have reported that vegetarians usually have lower serum cholesterol and triglyceride levels than nonvegetarians; at least one study showed that a group of male California Seventh-day Adventists (who are lacto-ovo-vegetarians) suffered their first heart attack a full decade later than most Americans, and their incidence of heart disease was only 60 percent of that of the average California male population. It is also of interest that vegetarians usually weigh less — more closely approaching their "ideal" weight — than do meat eaters.

Another consideration relates to the indigestible residues found in fruits, vegetables, and grains. These residues — referred to as fiber, roughage, bulk, or cellulose — contribute little or nothing of nutritional value but are exceedingly necessary for the proper functioning of the lower intestinal tract and for the formation of feces and the prevention of constipation. It has also been observed that the incidence of cancer of the colon is lower in populations where the diet is based on coarse cereals with a high fiber content. Eating bran cereal is one way of introducing fiber into your diet. Another is to increase your use of whole-grain flours and cereals while cutting back on the highly processed foods that are so common in the American diet.

By and large, vegetarians are healthy people, suffering from nutritional deficiencies no more — and in some instances, less — than others. If, however, dairy products are avoided in addition to meat, great care is needed to avoid deficiencies in vitamin B_{12}, riboflavin, iron, zinc, and calcium. Vitamin D could also be a problem for children not adequately exposed to sunlight. One of the biggest problems, however, is to obtain all the necessary amino acids, especially during growth periods.

AMINO ACIDS

Protein supplies the amino acids necessary for growth and tissue maintenance. The body requires a number of different amino acids and, within limits, can actually convert one amino acid into another. There are, however, several amino acids that the body cannot make itself and must obtain from the diet. These are called the "essential amino acids."

There are eight essential amino acids required by adults; children require a ninth during growth. Furthermore, since the body has no mechanism for the storage of individual amino acids, all the essential amino acids must be present at the same meal or within a very brief time interval for any one of them to do its proper job.

The quality of a particular food as a protein source is related not only to its digestibility and absorption but also to whether it contains all the essential amino acids. At the top of the list of quality protein foods is the egg; next comes milk. Both egg and milk proteins can furnish all the amino acids essential for normal growth and healthy life processes, provided they are eaten in sufficient amounts.

Fish, meat, and poultry are also quality protein sources. Of distinctly lower quality are the plant proteins such as those in wheat, corn, rice, beans, and nuts. These plant proteins may contain all the necessary amino acids, but in each one or more of the essential amino acids is present in such inadequate amounts that the entire protein value is diminished. The deficient amino acid is sometimes referred to as the "limiting" amino acid — that is, it limits the body's utilization of the protein. There is a way around this problem, however.

If a protein food is missing or is low in one or more of the essential amino acids, the deficiency can be corrected by eating another food that contains the missing elements. This process is called "mutual supplementation" or "protein complementarity." In general, legumes and leafy vegetables (for example, peas, beans, lentils, peanuts, greens) quite adequately supplement grains (wheat, oats, corn, rye, barley, rice). But if your diet merely omits animal flesh but includes dairy products, all of the essential amino acids will most probably be supplied without your having to worry about it. If dairy products are also avoided, care must be taken to avoid serious nutritional problems. It should also be remembered that nutritional requirements are greatly accentuated by illness. There is an excessive breakdown of body protein, as well as a depletion of other vital nutrients during febrile illnesses and after injuries, burns, or surgery.

A general rule of thumb is that if 70 percent of the protein in the diet comes from wheat protein and 30 percent comes from milk, yeast, nuts, soybeans, and other legumes, there will be excellent supplementary action. Of interest to those who avoid dairy products is the fact that a mixture of soy and sesame proteins has a high nutritive value, comparable to milk proteins.

Milk normally supplies 75 percent of the calcium, 43 percent of the riboflavin, 22 percent of the protein, and practically 100 percent of the vitamin B_{12} in the diet. One way for the total vegetarian to obtain an adequate intake of these nutrients is to use sufficient quantities of fortified soybean milk. For an adult, this would mean about two glasses a day. The label should be checked to make sure the soybean milk is fortified. Otherwise, a vitamin supplement is probably called for.

VITAMIN B_{12}

When all animal products — meat, eggs, milk, cheese, and so forth — are eliminated from the diet, the diet will not provide any vitamin B_{12}, since this vitamin is found in only the most minute quantities in some plants. This is of critical concern because a vitamin B_{12} deficiency can give rise to pernicious anemia (among other things) which, if not treated, can lead to serious illness and death. Vitamin B_{12} supplements usually are recommended in total vegetarian diets.

Why then do Hindu vegetarians, who eat no animal products at all, not have vitamin B_{12} deficiency problems? Unintentional contamination with animal products is probably the explanation. Parts of insects or their eggs or soil microorganisms get into the foods during growth or storage. Insects are not only a source of animal protein, but of vitamins such as B_{12} as well.

Another potential problem relates to the increased use of vitamin C. A recently published report suggests that the high doses of vitamin C (0.5 gram or more) popularly used as a home remedy against the common cold may destroy substantial amounts of vitamin B_{12}.

RIBOFLAVIN

Though intestinal bacteria probably manufacture small amounts of riboflavin, milk supplies about 43 percent of all the riboflavin consumed by most Americans. Eggs are also a good source of this vitamin. If dairy products and eggs are excluded from the diet, liberal amounts of leafy vegetables, asparagus, broccoli, okra, winter squash, and dried beans or peas must be eaten to meet daily requirements. Fortunately, riboflavin is relatively stable in heat and only slightly soluble in cooking water. Thus excessive losses of this vitamin during ordinary cooking are minimized.

CALCIUM

A large serving of about one cup of greens such as collards, kale, turnip, and mustard provides as much calcium as one cup of milk.

Cabbage, broccoli, and cauliflower will contribute lesser amounts of calcium but more than most other vegetables. Other plant sources that are moderate-to-good sources of calcium include legumes, particularly soybeans; some nuts, particularly almonds; and dried fruits. It must be remembered, however, that occasional use of these foods cannot be counted on to replace the calcium and riboflavin of milk.

IRON

Excluding meat and shellfish, the following are good sources of iron, in decreasing order of excellence: egg yolk, dried beans and other legumes, dried fruits, nuts, green leafy vegetables, whole-grain and enriched cereals and cereal products, and dark molasses. Milk is a poor source of iron.

ZINC

Zinc is present minimally in fruits, vegetables, and refined foods. Oysters are an unusually rich source. Whole grains are your best bet, followed by dry legumes and nuts.

VITAMIN D

A city-dwelling vegetarian who avoids milk products will often require a vitamin D supplement. Egg yolks, fortified milk, fish oils, and liver are the usual sources of this nutrient. Sunshine acting on the skin causes formation of vitamin D in the body and is usually sufficient for an adult who spends a good deal of time outside. Supplementation is usually recommended for infants, children, and pregnant women.

The most important safeguard for vegetarians is variety in the diet. The greatest risk comes from undue reliance on a single plant food source. Legumes, particularly soybeans, are rich in protein, B-vitamins, and iron. Grains are good sources of carbohydrates, proteins, thiamin, iron, and trace minerals. Nuts and other seeds contribute fat, protein, B-vitamins, and iron. Dark green, leafy vegetables are sources of calcium, riboflavin, and carotene — a precursor of vitamin A — and should be used liberally by total vegetarians.

2

A Trip to Your
Local Natural Foods Store

A TRIP TO YOUR
LOCAL NATURAL FOODS STORE

If you have never visited a natural foods store, there are many reasons to make your first trip:

1. The selection of grains and other natural food stuffs is unlikely to be equaled by any supermarket
2. You can readily find foods that contain few or no chemical additives
3. The personnel are usually polite and helpful
4. You're likely to meet some very interesting people

This is not to say that all natural foods stores are pillars of virtue or wisdom. Like all businesses, some are good and some are bad. Without question, some stores offer overpriced products with supposedly near magic properties. Also without question, many people go to such stores hoping to find foods with supernatural powers capable of curing or warding off almost every ailment known to people, from the common cold to cancer. To brand all natural foods storekeepers as charlatans and all their customers as fanatics would, however, be an insult to their integrity and to our intelligence.

Americans have one of the best food supplies in the world. Yet it is a sad commentary that, in many towns, the natural foods store is the only place that you can find items such as soybeans, bean sprouts, cracked wheat, rye flour, and, in many instances, even whole-wheat flour. It is also likely to be the only place where you can find cheese without artificial coloring or a selection of products without preservatives or other additives. How often have you eaten or even seen natural white cheese?

I can still remember my first visit to a natural foods store. Luckily I was directed to a very reputable place — one which offered a large variety of items (most of which I did not recognize!). It is not uncommon in such food stores to be expected to serve yourself, so I was able to browse around for quite some time.

It was a fascinating place. There was barrel after barrel of non-perishable foodstuffs ranging from alfalfa seeds (at the time I had no idea what they were) to whole-wheat noodles. On the shelves there were teas of every variety, as well as displays of cane sugar, cold-pressed vegetable oils, carob powder, and dried fruits. One section of the store contained a fascinating collection of cookbooks and free recipes, while another displayed an awesome selection of vitamins and minerals. Spices were dispensed from gallon-sized jars into small paper packets, while cheese was cut to order and honey was ladled into your own container. The dairy section proffered fresh eggs, brewer's yeast, and wheat germ. Meat was nowhere in sight. Hanging scales were placed at strategic points throughout the store. You were expected to scoop out, weigh, package, and mark your own wares. No one checked you; trust was clearly the order of the day. Near the entrance were yogurt makers and fresh dark bread, while in the back were beads and shells for making your own jewelry. A very, very hard place to leave.

Finally I decided on a few items: whole-wheat noodles, because I at least recognized their shape; pita bread, which I had learned to love in Egypt; carob powder, because I had read somewhere that it was a good substitute for chocolate; and fresh cashews, because I felt that I deserved a treat. It was not until a later trip that I worked up my nerve to purchase alfalfa seeds and bulgur. I was terrified that someone was going to ask me for my favorite recipe for those ingredients! As it turned out, the only thing that I was asked was whether I had brought my own shopping bag or would I like to borrow one of theirs.

I have since learned to ask for help and to not feel that I should know it all. That, however, is easier said now than it was done then.

MENU-PLANNING HINTS

When trying out a new idea, such as vegetarian cooking, there is a great temptation to run out and buy a little bit of everything and then to try and tackle a menu replete with new dishes. Try and control yourself! One new recipe is probably all that your patience and palate can cope with at any one time. A different side dish may be the place to start. At this point, I have to confess that this is not the way I did it. I not only went out and loaded up at the natural foods store, but I then came home so sure that I would remember the identity of each item that I didn't bother to label any of them. I'm sure that you can guess how this tale ended.

When you do move on to serving an entire meatless meal, don't be constrained by your old pattern of one main dish served with minor accompaniments. In vegetarian cooking, there's no reason for any dish to take a back seat. When I have the time, I often make multiple complementary dishes — a vegetarian smorgasbord. Sometimes, however, one dish is such a favorite that the only thing to do is serve it alone or accompanied at most by a hot bread and maybe some cheese.

SHOPPING TIPS

Following is a description of a number of items that you are likely to find in a natural foods store. I have also worked in a few hints for better health.

Acerola powder. Acerola is a fruit, related to the cherry, that grows in the West Indies. A half cup of acerola juice contains almost thirty times the amount of vitamin C as does the same amount of orange juice.

Agar-agar. A seaweed with thickening qualities, used like gelatin to make molded salads and desserts. Comes in flakes, powder, or stick form.

Alfalfa seeds. Tiny black seeds which are easily sprouted, making an excellent alternative to lettuce in sandwiches.

Barley. This grain is usually "pearled" to remove the tenacious hull. The whiter the barley, the greater the pearling and, hence, the greater the loss of nutrients. The darker barley usually found in natural foods stores is often referred to as "hulled barley."

Bean flakes. These beans have been partially cooked and flattened, thus greatly reducing the cooking time when they are used as cereals or in soups, casseroles, and so forth. Flaking loosens the beans' skins, causing them to rise to the top in cooking; just stir them back in.

Black beans. A variety of soybeans, these small oval beans have black skins and white interiors, and have been long popular in Mexico and the Southwest. They are also known as turtle soup beans. Black beans and rice, a traditional recipe, is an excellent example of "protein complementarity."

Blackstrap molasses. A product of the last extraction of the sugarcane, blackstrap molasses contains calcium, iron, and most of the B vitamins, and is slightly lower in calories than sugar or honey.

Bran. A part of the wheat berry that is removed as the whole wheat is milled and "refined." A great source of dietary fiber.

Brewer's yeast. As the name suggests, this yeast is associated with the brewing of beer. It is also a good source of B vitamins, amino acids, and minerals and could be used as a source of these nutrients should your diet be deficient in these areas.

Brown rice. A whole-grain rice, as opposed to white rice which has been stripped of its bran and many of its nutrients.

Buckwheat. A whole grain that is very carefully hulled and graded. The best is groats, which are the whole buckwheat grains. Grinding the whole-grain buckwheat produces a dark flour with a rich taste.

Bulgur. You will probably find this ingredient spelled a number of different ways: *bulghur, bulgar, burghul.* And occasionally bulgur will be referred to as cracked wheat. Though bulgur and cracked wheat are usually interchangeable in recipes, there is a difference between the two. Both bulgur and cracked wheat are whole-grain wheats which have been cracked, but bulgur has also been parboiled and then dried, whereas cracked wheat has not been cooked and, thus, requires a slightly longer preparation time. Bulgur also comes "refined" and "nonrefined." The former is lighter in color and takes a slightly shorter time to soften than the unrefined variety. Bulgur has a delicate nutlike flavor and is a staple of Middle Eastern households.

Carob powder. Also known as St. John's Bread, carob powder is an excellent substitute for chocolate, though its taste is not really comparable. Not only is carob much lower in calories than chocolate or cocoa, it contains almost no fat, is a relatively good source of protein, and contains none of the stimulants found in chocolate. In substituting carob powder for chocolate, 3 tablespoons of carob powder plus 2 tablespoons of water or milk equals 1 square of chocolate. Carob powder is obtained from the beans of the carob tree, grown in the Mediterranean area and in the Middle East.

Cheese. If you're trying to control cholesterol, fats, and calories, it will affect your choice of cheeses. You will want to look for cheeses made from skim milk: 1 percent- to 2 percent-fat cottage cheese, farmer cheese, pot cheese, ricotta. Parmesan cheese, mozzarella, Port du Salut, or other cheeses made from partial skim milk are your next best choice.

Chick peas. These legumes are also known as garbanzo beans. They are very light brown in color, have a nutlike flavor, and are a traditional food in the Middle East.

Cornmeal. Coarsely ground whole white or yellow corn. White cornmeal is sweeter and lighter than yellow cornmeal.

Couscous. A cracked, uncooked wheat resembling semolina. A traditional North African wheat dish.

Cracked wheat. See Bulgur.

Date sugar. Made from dried, pulverized dates.

Dried fruit. Sometimes drier than the commercial varieties, but free from chemical preservatives. Some are honey dipped for natural preservation.

Fertile eggs. So-called because roosters are usually kept with the hens. These "barnyard" hens are allowed to run loose, thus obtaining a more "natural" diet.

Garbanzos. Another name for chick peas.

Granola. A mixture of flaked grains, seeds, nuts, and fruits; easily made at home.

Groats. Whole buckwheat grains. Also known as kasha.

Honey. Light honey is fragrant, delicate, and sweet. Dark honey is pungent and aromatic.

Kasha. Another name for buckwheat groats. A staple in the Russian and Eurasian diet.

Kelp. A seaweed rich in iodine and other nutrients. Powdered kelp is often used in place of salt.

Lecithin. A fatlike substance found commonly in foods and also available as a dietary supplement. Widely touted as being effective in lowering serum cholesterol, but evidence does not support this claim.

Lentils. Small, flat, dirty-brown dried beans. They cook in a relatively short time and are excellent in soups, casseroles, and meatless burgers. An even smaller lentil, bright orange, is used in Indian cooking.

Meat. No, you probably won't find meat in a natural foods store, but since I'm not trying to convince you to become a vegetarian but am only offering you some new recipes, a few words about meat seem in order. If you're interested in reducing your fat, cholesterol, and caloric intakes, you might want to consider using lean meats (fish, chicken, turkey, and veal) more often than beef, lamb, pork, and ham. You will also want to keep to a minimum your use of organ meats, such as chicken livers and shellfish. The American Heart Association also suggests that you limit your egg yolk intake (the whites are not a problem) to three yolks a week.

Milk powder. Milk powder offers two major advantages over fresh milk: it stores for long periods of time and, if you buy nonfat dry milk, it is cheaper serving-for-serving than whole milk. A glass of whole fluid milk usually costs three times as much as a glass of reconstituted nonfat dry milk. Milk protects your calcium, phosphorus, magnesium, vitamins A, D, B_{12}, and riboflavin reserves, as well as providing protein. In skim milk, only the fat is missing; most of the nutrients are still there, but at a great caloric saving (85 calories per cup of skim milk versus 165 calories per cup for whole milk). If you don't care for the taste of skim or nonfat dry milk for drinking, you can mix it with equal parts of regular milk or use it for cooking. Dry milk powder comes in two forms: instant and noninstant. Both are nutritionally sound and the instant powder certainly mixes more easily with liquids than does the noninstant variety, but the latter form seems to work better for cooking. Incidentally, despite its name, buttermilk is not fat-laden. One cup of buttermilk contains only 90 calories.

Millet. This grain is sometimes known as "poor man's rice," though it is not as flavorful as rice or wheat. Millet is used heavily in China, Japan, and Africa. It is best when mixed with other ingredients.

Miso. A paste made from soybeans, barley, and fermented rice.

Mung beans. Small, greenish beans which are easily sprouted. The sprouts are somewhat sharper in taste and larger in size than alfalfa sprouts and, personally, I don't care for them raw though I do enjoy them when stir-fried with other vegetables.

Nuts. You'll probably find a variety of raw and toasted nuts and, miracle of miracles, most have not been salted.

Oats. Oats are carefully hulled to remove the last bits of hull that tend to cling to the crease in the grain. Usually used in the form of rolled oats, though whole oats may be used like barley.

Papaya syrup. A concentrate made from ripened papaya, used in desserts, drinks, and sauces.

Pinto beans. These brown-speckled beans are a favorite in the South and Southwest.

Protein/vitamin/mineral supplements. When time, money, illness, or anything else prevent you from meeting your nutrient requirements through a variety of foods, you may want to consider a protein and/or vitamin-mineral supplement. When purchased by generic name as opposed to a brand name, supplements will be cheaper but equally effective. Just compare the labels carefully to make sure that you're getting what you want. It is important to remember, however, that just because a little may be good for you doesn't mean that a lot is necessarily better. Many nutrient supplements are dangerous when taken in high doses.

Raw sugar. Sugar that has not been bleached. Use as you would regular sugar.

Rice-wine vinegar. A delicate vinegar made from rice and imported from Japan.

Rye. A mild-tasting grain which comes flaked or ground into grits or flour. When the flour is used in making bread, it is usually mixed with whole-wheat flour as the rye tends to be heavy.

Vegetable broth powder. A fine powder made from dehydrated vegetables and sometimes fortified with yeast or wheat germ. When combined with water or milk, it makes an excellent soup or sauce base or stock for cooking grains or beans.

Sea salt. Sea salt is solar evaporated and then kiln dried. Preferred by many because of its natural trace minerals content.

And now for a commercial! If I had to pick one food-related warning over all others, I would urge moderation in the use of salt, regardless of its source. A heavy use of salt is associated with an increased likelihood of high blood pressure, causing difficulties for your heart and arteries. And, unfortunately, scientists estimate that Americans, on the average, consume daily approximately five times the amount of salt that is considered desirable. Won't you at least taste your food before salting it?

You will find that very few of the recipes in this book call for the addition of salt, though I have made no attempt to keep the recipes salt-free. After all, there are practically no naturally salt-free foods available, and most commercially prepared items have salt added to them. Soy sauce, bouillon cubes, and broth granules are excessively salty, as are most of the prepared steak and barbecue sauces.

When you do buy salt, check its iodine content. Most of the iodine, an essential nutrient in our diet, comes through the use of table salt.

Sea vegetables. Dried seaweeds which come in a variety of forms and names; wakame, nori, dulse, and kelp are the best known.

Sesame seeds. An excellent source of protein, calcium, magnesium, and unsaturated fatty acids. Sesame seeds have many uses, and are often made into sesame butter.

Soft wheat. Lower in protein and in gluten than hard winter wheat and, therefore, is most suitable for grinding into pastry flour.

Soybeans. Excellent source of quality protein and unsaturated fat. Whole, they require an extensive soaking and cooking period. Soybean flakes and granules require significantly less preparation time. Almost guaranteed to cause flatulence in the novice bean eater!

Spices. Though premixed combinations of herbs and spices are readily available, it's really more fun — and more economical — to make your own.

Split peas. These dried and split green peas are especially good in soups.

Sunflower seeds. These are not just for the birds. When hulled and toasted, they are a great snack and a delicious addition to granola cereal.

Tahini. Sesame seeds which have been crushed to form a versatile paste.

Tamari. Soy sauce made of soybeans, wheat, and salt. Often used instead of plain salt for seasoning. Very salty.

Teas. You will find a great variety of herbal teas. Some of the more popular are: clover blossom, lemon grass, rose hips, spearmint, camomile, and raspberry leaf. Some herbal teas are much higher in vitamin C content than is orange juice; rose hip tea is one of these. Vitamin C is very unstable in the presence of heat, however.

Tiger's milk. A dietary supplement in powdered form, tiger's milk comes plain or flavored. Made from nonfat dry milk, soybeans, and yeast, tiger's milk is comparable to nonfat dry milk in nutrient value, though it is somewhat higher in protein and phosphorous and considerably higher in calcium.

Tofu. A cheeselike curd made from soybeans.

Triticale. A fairly new grain variety, triticale was originally a cross between durham wheat, hard red winter wheat, and rye. It is slightly higher in protein and has a better balance of amino acids than some other grains. Available whole, flaked, and as a flour.

Turtle soup beans. Another name for black beans.

VegeBurger. A meat substitute made from soybeans, wheat, and vegetables.

Vegetable oils. Almost all oils, including some labeled "cold pressed," are made by heating the grains, beans, or seeds before the oils are extracted. Commercial processors also use chemical solvents to extract the oils. In contrast, unrefined oils are heated and then pressed without the use of any chemicals or solvents. Unrefined oils will smell quite different to those used to highly refined oils. Additionally, most unrefined oils should not be heated over 350° F. Care should be taken to keep untreated vegetable oils in a cool, dry place to help prevent them from becoming rancid.

Another health note. Excessive amounts of fats, especially saturated fats, may be dangerous to your long-term health. They often contribute to elevated cholesterol levels which, when combined with other undesirable life-style features such as excessive sugar and salt intake, persistent overweight, tension, cigarette smoking, and inactivity, set the stage for the development of heart disease.

The easiest way to remember which fats are saturated and which are unsaturated is to keep in mind that, in general, saturated fats are solid at room temperature (butter, fats in meat, coconut oil, cocoa butter), whereas unsaturated fats are liquid at room temperature (most vegetable oils). What about margarine? Vegetable oils can be turned into solids through saturation. Unless the product is labeled, you will not know what percentage of the margarine is saturated and how much remains unsaturated. An artificially saturated product has absolutely no advantages over a naturally saturated product. A saturated fat is a saturated fat, regardless of how it got that way.

In recipes calling for vegetable oil, safflower oil will be your best choice, followed by soybean, corn, cottonseed, sesame, and sunflower oils. Olive oil should be used sparingly — only when a real taste difference can be detected — and the same is true for butter. As for margarine, look for one that lists a *liquid* vegetable oil as its first ingredient. And, as you might expect, tub margarines tend to be less saturated than stick margarines as they are not required to hold a rigid form.

Wheat germ. This heart of the wheat kernel is rich in essential nutrients, and has a variety of uses. It is available raw or toasted. Toasted wheat germ is the tastier, to my way of thinking. Toasting also increases its shelf life; raw wheat germ is not very stable and must be stored in the refrigerator to keep its oil from becoming rancid.

Whole grain flakes. Like the bean flakes, these are grains that have been partially cooked and flattened. They are dry, light in weight, and more tender than whole or cracked grains.

Whole-wheat berries. These are the whole-wheat grains which have not been flaked, cracked, or ground.

Whole-wheat flour. A hard winter wheat that has been ground into a light brown flour. Stone-ground whole-wheat flour is one of the most versatile flours around.

Whole-wheat pastry flour. A ground whole-grain soft wheat. This light flour is great for flaky pie crusts or any other recipe where you might ordinarily use white flour. Sifted whole-wheat flour may be used in place of whole-wheat pastry flour.

Yogurt. Not only does yogurt have a pleasantly tart taste, but it can also often be consumed and tolerated by people who otherwise suffer discomfort from the ingestion of milk. Yogurt is very easy to make at home.

CHAPTER
3

Food Additives
and Pesticides

FOOD ADDITIVES AND PESTICIDES

ADDITIVES VERSUS ADULTERATION

Resourceful entrepreneurs have long practiced adulteration when quantity was more rewarding than quality. If a particular product was scarce and expensive, merchants had to find some way of increasing the quantity and reducing the price, usually by bulking out the genuine article with a cheap extender. The extender might or might not be harmful. In the early nineteenth century, for example, pepper was routinely adulterated with comparatively innocuous materials such as mustard husks, pea flour, juniper berries, and a commodity known as "pepper dust," which appears to have consisted of the sweepings of the storeroom floor. On the other hand, fake varieties of green China tea were often produced from thorn leaves by drying them and then coloring them with verdigris, a highly poisonous substance.

Other pleasantries from the "good old days" included sand in the sugar, water in the milk, plaster of paris in the bread, and vitriol in the beer. "Crusted old port" was no more than new port crusted with a layer of supertartrate of potash, while table wine derived its "nutty" flavor from bitter almonds, which contain prussic acid. Pickles owed their appetizing green color to copper, the rainbow hues of sweets and candies were produced by the highly poisonous salts of copper and lead, and the rind of Gloucester cheese frequently acquired its rich orange color from additives of red lead. Commercial bread was loaded with alum, coffee was diluted with chicory or acorns, and cocoa powder often contained a large percentage of brick dust.

Public complaints led finally to governmental intervention, and in 1860 the first British Food and Drugs Act was passed. Though "states rights" laws dealing with the regulation of food and drugs date back to colonial times, the first national food and drug law for the United States was passed in 1906.

TODAY'S "ADDITIVES"

By 1938 we had the Federal Food, Drug and Cosmetic Act, which was amended significantly between 1954 and 1960 as a result of deliberations by the Delaney Committee of the House of Representatives. These amendments applied the principle that the safety of pesticides and food and color additives should be determined before the public is exposed to them. The burden of proof was shifted from the government to the manufacturer, the government being responsible for evaluating the evidence submitted.

Early in the deliberations that led to some of the amendments of the 1938 Act, it became clear that chemicals in foods would have to be regulated in at least two separate categories: pesticides, which were used on raw agricultural commodities; and food additives, which were substances added to improve food products or to facilitate processing or packaging. One wonders if the insects, rodent droppings, mold, and other debris sometimes found in food shouldn't be considered another class of additives!

PESTICIDES

The Pesticide Chemicals Amendment, which became law in 1954, was designed to protect the general public from the harm of poisonous residue without banning the use of pesticides completely. The law calls for joint responsibility, requiring the Food and Drug Administration (FDA) to give an advisory opinion on the safety of the proposed use of a pesticide before the Agriculture Department certifies the pesticide for use.

Once a pesticide is certified for use, the FDA sets the amount of residue allowed ("tolerance") to remain on vegetables, fruits, meats, and other foods. The tolerance figure is arrived at primarily by observing what the chemicals do to animals, and then setting the level considerably below that which causes observable damage to the animals. Products are to be monitored, and those found to contain levels of pesticides above that permitted by regulation are supposed to be seized and taken off the market. This raises a number of issues and problems.

Though an attempt is made to adjust the tolerances to take into consideration multiple chemical ingestations (that is, not just the chemical being tested, but others taken in by way of other foods, polluted air and water, cigarette smoke, drugs, etc.), many question the safety of these tolerances. Additionally, there is the problem of trying to monitor 900 separate pesticide chemicals, which are combined into 45,000 different pesticide products, one-half of which are used in and around the home. Rachel Carson, in her book *Silent Spring*, sums up the feeling of many when she suggests that the very idea of setting a tolerance for chemicals known to be harmful is questionable — "deliberately poisoning our food, then policing the result."

Critics of widespread indiscriminate use of pesticides point out that chemicals which can kill insects and plant pests can also have an effect on animals and humans, and should be more carefully controlled. The safety of tolerance levels should be clearly established and adherence to those levels strictly enforced, a responsibility not being fulfilled adequately at present.

In the words of a past FDA Commissioner: "Our principal concern here is not with our present regulatory methods, but with the fact that in many parts of the world pesticides are poorly controlled, if controlled at all. If all pesticides become ubiquitous, as did DDT, and if raw materials and finished foods are to move easily across borders, then the hazards from pesticides may increase dramatically." At present, however, the greatest danger to the general public is probably improper use of pesticides in and around the house.

Over the years, a number of innovative nonchemical pesticides have proved effective, but chemical pesticides usually have proved to be cheaper and more rapidly applied. One wonders, however, whether alternative means would not be developed if our great scientific technology was forced to focus on the problem.

FOOD ADDITIVES

The Food Additives Amendment was approved in 1958, and the Color Additive Amendments in 1960. Like the Pesticide Amendment, the intent was not to ban the use of food chemicals but to ensure their safety when used. Food additives are defined as substances added directly to food, or substances which may reasonably be expected to become components of food through surface contact with equipment or packaging materials, or even substances that may otherwise affect the food without becoming a part of it (such as various forms of radiation used in food processing). There are a number of substances (better than 700) added to food which are not legally classified as food additives and are, therefore, exempt from the premarketing clearance requirements. These substances are classified as "generally regarded as safe" (GRAS).

To appear on the GRAS list, a substance must be shown to be safe through "scientific procedures," or the substance must be considered generally recognized as safe merely because of a history of its use in food with no recognized associated toxic ill effects. There are, thus, many additives in common use that have never been tested adequately for safety, except perhaps for acute toxicity, because they were in existence long before the Food Additives Amendment of 1958 was conceived. Additionally, an increasing spectrum of consumers and scientists are questioning whether additives that have come on the market since 1958 are being adequately screened — especially for long-term effects such as genetic damage.

In a very real sense, one cannot test for absolute safety but only for the presence of known hazards. Even if a substance passed the most rigorous testing for safety today, new scientific knowledge and testing capabilities may unearth tomorrow a previously unrecognized and undetectable hazard.

About three-fifths of food additives are artificial flavors and colors, emulsifiers, stabilizers, and thickeners whose main purpose is to make foods more attractive. This function may well be challenged, but if these additives make nutritious foods look and taste appealing, if without them such foods would not find wide acceptance, they may be as beneficial as the preservatives, antioxidants, leaveners, antistaling, and mold-retarding agents that help protect the consumer from bacteria and toxins. One nutritionist predicts that by the early 1980s, one-fifth of the "meats" in American diets will be fabricated from soybeans, peanuts, and cottonseed. Certainly, sophisticated use of chemistry will be needed to give these new unconventional foodstuffs acceptable tastes and textures.

It is true, however, that many additives used in the past for valid reasons could probably be eliminated now, at least in the more developed countries. For example, in this day of mass food production and rapid refrigerated transport systems, spoilage is not the problem that it was once. Some additives whose inclusion was approved when conditions were less favorable could be eliminated, and better sanitary conditions during processing could eliminate others. On the other hand, if using certain additives to minimize spoilage and extend shelf-life helps keep food production costs down, this could benefit both industry and consumer. Judging from current food prices, however, it is difficult to believe that any of these "savings" are being passed along to the public.

EXTRANEOUS MATTER

Keeping food 100 percent pure is virtually impossible, and the health regulations in this country allow a certain amount of "filth" in foods. Though these unintentional "additives" are not considered to be harmful to your health, many find distressing the thought of rodent hairs or insects ground up in their bread. Of itself, a rodent hair or roach fragment or fly leg hardly constitutes an imminent threat to health. But when found in food, it is evidence of possible contamination by disease organisms. It is true, of course, that disease organisms are often washed out or destroyed during processing and cooking preparations, but rodents and vermin do not always obligingly deposit their filth before the final cooking stage. Infestation may well occur during the cooling period before the food is sealed or packaged.

Many food processors follow more exacting purity standards than those demanded by the FDA; others, unfortunately, do not meet the FDA standards of sanitary practice. In 1972, General Accounting Office auditors accompanied FDA personnel to food plants in twenty-one states. Of ninety-seven plants selected at random, only thirty met FDA standards; twenty-three plants were judged to have serious unsanitary conditions; twenty-eight were judged to have minor unsanitary conditions, considered not sufficient to contaminate the product or endanger human health; the other sixteen fell somewhere between serious and minor.

Following publication of the General Accounting Office report, Congress increased the FDA's food policing budget, but individual plant inspection will still probably not occur, on the average, more than once every three to four years.

HAZARDS AND PRIORITIES

It might be interesting to look at the six broad areas of hazards identified and given priority by the FDA:

Food-borne infection is ranked number one because of its continuing widespread incidence and because of the high risk in some instances, such as botulism. It is predicted that the hazards of food-borne infection will increase as foods are synthesized, as they are manufactured in one place, consumed in others, and stored and moved repeatedly. Further, it may be that contaminating organisms will become more and more resistant to available antibiotics, thus increasing the hazard of gastroenteritis and more serious infections.

Malnutrition. Biochemically provable nutritional deficiencies do occur in numbers sufficient to be of concern now, and when a larger part of our food supply is manufactured, the problems may increase. We do not know everything that should be included in artificially constituted foods, or in what amounts, to make these analogs the nutritional equal of traditional foods.

Environmental contaminants may or may not be from industrial sources. Mercury poisoning has been both industrial and natural. But the increasing pollution of our world, the recycling of valuable resources such as animal wastes, and the new uses of previously discarded products such as sewage will increase still further the risk of serious hazard from environmental sources.

Naturally occurring toxicants are also likely to be concentrated as we process and manufacture foods, and likely to survive future manufacturing processes that ignore the potential of this hazard. Many commonly consumed legumes contain toxic materials as part of their normal composition. These foods are now safe for consumption only because the toxic materials are destroyed by cooking. At present, says the FDA, our best safeguard against this class of hazard is to adhere to traditional methods of food preparation and consumption, rather than to experiment too boldly with novel methods of preparation.

Pesticide residues are distinguished from the earlier category of industrial environmental contaminants primarily because of their toxicity. Of major concern is the possibility of inadequate worldwide control of these substances.

Food additives rank sixth in the FDA's list of hazards, "mostly because so much is known about many of them, and all are now, and surely will continue to be, well regulated."

Recipes

CHAPTER

4

The Basics — Only Better!

THE BASICS — ONLY BETTER!

Foods are blended with spices, flavorings, and dressings for greater variety. You will find many uses for these basics in your cooking, especially in this book, so I have put them right up front.

These recipes are not only tastier than their store-bought look-alikes, but they also allow you to control the individual ingredients. If you tend to read a cookbook like a novel, as I do, you will begin making these recipes now, in time to have them for the main portions of the book.

SPICE MIXTURES

There are many spice combinations that tend to recur in recipes. For example, there are combinations of oregano and basil in tomato dishes, turmeric and coriander in curries, and pepper and cinnamon in Middle Eastern foods. The commercial mixtures are not as fresh and no where near as much fun as the ones you can mix up yourself.

Middle Eastern Spice

2 teaspoons paprika
2 teaspoons ground cinnamon
1 teaspoon cayenne pepper
1 teaspoon ground cloves

1 teaspoon ground nutmeg
1 teaspoon ground cardamom
1 teaspoon ground cumin

1. Mix well.

2. Store in a jar with a tight-fitting lid.

Aromatic Salt

¼ cup dried savory
¼ cup chopped dried parsley
2 tablespoons dried thyme leaves
1 tablespoon dried sage
2 tablespoons celery seed
2 teaspoons dried grated lemon rind
1 cup iodized salt or sea salt

1. Crush and grind the ingredients thoroughly.

2. Store the salt in a jar with a tight-fitting top, transferring small amounts to your salt shaker as needed.

Curry Powder

1 teaspoon dry mustard
2 teaspoons black mustard seeds (optional)
1 tablespoon turmeric
2 teaspoons ground coriander
1 teaspoon each ground cumin, cayenne pepper, ground cardamom,
    ground cinnamon, and ground ginger
1 tablespoon fenugreek (optional)

1. Mix ingredients together well.

2. Store in a tightly closed jar.

Note: For a hotter curry, add ½ teaspoon ground black pepper and ½ teaspoon dried chili pepper to the mix.

Italian Seasoning

1 tablespoon dried oregano
1 tablespoon chopped dried parsley
1 teaspoon each rosemary, thyme, paprika, and cracked black
    peppercorns
2 tablespoons dried basil

1. Reduce the ingredients to a fine powder in an electric blender, or just stir together well.

2. Store in a jar with a tight-fitting lid.

Lemon Pepper

2 tablespoons cracked black peppercorns
1 tablespoon grated lemon rind

1. Combine together well.

2. Store the pepper in a container with a tight-fitting lid.

Salad Herbs

2 tablespoons each chopped dried chives, and parsley
1 tablespoon each dried basil and dried savory
1 teaspoon each dried tarragon and dried mint

1. Combine the ingredients well.

2. Store in a tightly covered container.

Chili Powder

2½ tablespoons ground cumin
¾ teaspoon dried chili pepper
⅜ teaspoon cayenne pepper
3 teaspoons dried oregano
½ teaspoon dry mustard
1 teaspoon celery seeds
½ teaspoon ground cinnamon
¼ teaspoon ground cloves

1. Grind the spices to a fine powder.

2. Store the chili powder in a tightly covered jar.

Note: You might want to add some garlic powder at the time of cooking.

Conserie D'Harissa

6 tablespoons cayenne pepper
3 tablespoons ground cumin
⅜ teaspoon caraway seeds

½ teaspoon ground cardamom
½ teaspoon ground coriander

1. Grind the spices together.

2. Store the spices in a jar with a tight-fitting lid.

Preheated Oil

Vegetable oil
1 small slice fresh gingerroot
Green onion, leek, or scallion

1. Heat the oil to about 300 degrees — no higher.

2. Add the remaining ingredients to the quantity desired. Turn off the heat and let the mixture bubble until the moisture is gone.

3. Cool the mixture, strain, and rebottle for use later.

FLAVORED BUTTERS

These delicious butters can be frozen and then sliced straight from the freezer, for use on cooked vegetables, or, if you eat it, then on poached fish. Softened, these butters are great for sandwiches, canapés, and toast. They are all prepared in the same way, so the first recipe has the directions for the remaining butters.

Parsley Butter

½ cup butter
2 tablespoons chopped fresh parsley

1 tablespoon lemon juice
Black pepper

1. Cream together all the ingredients. Using cool, wet hands, shape the butter into a roll about 1½ inches in diameter.

2. To freeze for later use, wrap the butter in foil or freezer paper and pack in a plastic bag. Seal tightly.

3. To serve, unwrap the frozen butter and slice into pieces using a knife dipped in hot water. Or, if time allows, soften the butter at room temperature.

Note: This is especially good with whitefish.

Herb Butter
(good over hot vegetables)

½ cup butter   2 tablespoons Salad Herbs (page 49)

Cheddar Butter
(something different for your vegetables)

½ cup butter   3 tablespoons fresh chives
½ cup grated cheddar cheese

Garlic Butter
(makes excellent garlic bread)

½ cup butter   Juice from 1 clove garlic
½ teaspoon Italian Seasoning (page 48)

Mustard Butter
(excellent for baked fish)

½ cup butter   1 tablespoon prepared hot mustard

Lemon Butter
(serve with fish or vegetables)

½ cup butter
2 teaspoons grated lemon rind
2 teaspoons lemon juice

Lime Butter
(a pleasant change from the taste of lemon)

½ cup butter
1 tablespoon chopped fresh parsley
2 tablespoons lime juice

Anchovy Butter
(delicious served with poached fish)

½ cup butter
2 teaspoons anchovy paste (very salty)
2 teaspoons finely chopped fresh parsley

LOW-FAT SUBSTITUTES

For those concerned with the high caloric content of the usual commercial items, here are a few ways around the problem. Also, for those watching their cholesterol, a recipe for a modified form of butter is included.

Mock Cream Cheese   Makes 2 cups

1½ cups low-fat cottage cheese   ¼ cup skim milk
¼ cup buttermilk

1. Combine all the ingredients in a blender and purée until very smooth.

2. Refrigerate. The mixture will thicken to a cream cheese consistency.

Mock Sour Cream I   Makes 2 cups
(for serving cold only)

1 cup buttermilk   2 teaspoons lemon juice
1 cup low-fat cottage cheese

1. Combine all the ingredients in a blender and purée until smooth.

2. Refrigerate until ready to serve.

Mock Sour Cream II   Makes 1½ cups
(for long-cooked dishes)

1 tablespoon vegetable oil
2 tablespoons all-purpose flour
1¼ cups buttermilk

⅛ teaspoon white pepper
2 teaspoons lemon juice

1. Heat the oil in a small saucepan. Add the flour and simmer for 1 or 2 minutes, stirring until bubbly.

2. Add the buttermilk gradually. Stir until thick and creamy. Season with pepper and lemon juice.

Mock Sour Cream III   Makes 1 cup
(for cooked dishes, added just before serving)

1 cup plain low-fat yogurt
1 tablespoon all-purpose flour

1 teaspoon mayonnaise (optional)

1. Combine the ingredients in a bowl and mix well.

2. Refrigerate until ready to use.

Mock Butter
(with the taste of butter)

Makes 5 cups

1 pound butter   1 cup vegetable oil

1. Blend well.

2. Refrigerate until ready to use.

No-Fat Salad Dressing

Makes 1½ cups

1 cup tomato juice or V-8
½ cup cider vinegar
1 teaspoon granulated sugar
Juice from 1 clove garlic
1 tablespoon Italian Seasoning (page 48)
⅛ teaspoon dry mustard
1½ tablespoons agar-agar

1. Blend the ingredients together well.

2. Refrigerate until ready to use.

Note: This tasty dressing contains no oil. The agar-agar thickens the mixture somewhat, adding body to the dressing that would otherwise be missing. You can substitute unflavored gelatin for the agar-agar.

Yogurt Mayonnaise

Makes 1 cup

1 large egg
½ teaspoon dry mustard
2 tablespoons cider vinegar or lemon juice
1 cup plain low-fat yogurt

1. In a blender, combine the egg, mustard, and vinegar with ¼ cup of the yogurt. Blend on low speed.

2. Uncover the blender and slowly add the remaining yogurt as the blender continues to run.

3. Refrigerate until ready to use.

Tofu Mayonnaise

Makes 1 cup

6 ounces tofu
2 tablespoons lemon juice
2 tablespoons olive oil

Dash of white pepper
Dash of dry mustard
1 tablespoon miso or ¼ teaspoon salt

1. Combine and purée all the ingredients in a blender.

2. Refrigerate until ready to use.

VINEGARS

Brandied Vinegar
(a delicately flavored vinegar)

Makes 2 quarts

4 cups distilled white vinegar
3 cups dry red or white wine
1 cup brandy
1 tablespoon dried or fresh tarragon leaves
6 whole cloves
1 tablespoon grated lemon rind
1 clove garlic, quartered
1 tablespoon fresh chopped chives

1. Combine all the ingredients in a saucepan. Simmer, covered, for 30 minutes.

2. Bottle the vinegar, tightly capped, and store in a cool place.

3. Strain the vinegar before using, or at least remove the cloves and garlic.

Note: Your choice of the type and color of the wine will obviously influence the final product.

Mint Vinegar   Makes 1 quart

4 cups cider vinegar
1 cup granulated sugar
2 cups chopped fresh spearmint leaves

1. Combine all the ingredients in a saucepan. Cook until the sugar is dissolved. Cool.

2. Bottle and cap the vinegar. Store it in a cool place for about a week.

3. Strain the vinegar before using.

Note: Good for use in light fruit punches or served, hot or cold, as a mint sauce.

Spicy Vinegar   Makes 1 quart

4 cups cider vinegar
2 tablespoons granulated sugar
4 tablespoons Curry Powder (page 48)
1 teaspoon celery seed

1. Combine all the ingredients in a saucepan. Cover and simmer for 30 minutes.

2. Pour the vinegar into a clean jar, cap tightly, and let stand in a cool place for about 2 weeks.

3. Strain the vinegar before using.

Wine Vinegar   Makes 1+ cup

1 cup unpasteurized wine vinegar, to serve as a starter
Dry red or white wine, or a combination

1. Pour the vinegar into a glass jar or bottle, or into a large crock. Add enough wine to fill. Cover the opening with a loose-fitting top or a piece of cheesecloth to allow for air circulation and to keep out the fruit flies that are invariably attracted to this tasty brew. Store at about 70 degrees.

2. After a month or so, draw off some of the vinegar and taste it. If you like the flavor, transfer some to a tightly sealed bottle. If the mixture is too wine-like, pour it back and let it continue to ferment. If the vinegar is too strong, dilute it with water when bottling it or when using it. Vinegar tends to mellow somewhat with aging.

3. To keep the process going, merely replace the drawn-off vinegar with more wine. Any tasty, but not necessarily expensive, wine will do the trick. However, do not use fortified wines such as sherry or port.

MARINADES

Bourbon Delight   Makes 1 cup

¼ cup bourbon
¼ cup Spicy Soy Sauce (page 72)
¼ cup prepared mustard
¼ cup brown sugar
1 small onion, thinly sliced

1. Combine all the ingredients in a bowl.

2. Refrigerate until ready to use.

Note: Try marinating cooked beans in this. It is good when the beans are used in a cold salad or when they are reheated.

Curry Marinade   Makes 1¼ cups
(good for vegetables that will be cooked)

¼ cup vegetable oil
1 tablespoon Curry Powder (page 48)
1 small onion, finely chopped
1 cup (or more) dry red or white wine

1. Combine the oil and curry powder in a skillet. Heat, stirring, until the mustard seeds "pop."

2. Add the onion and sauté for 5 minutes.

3. Stir in the wine and heat to lukewarm. The marinade is now ready to pour over vegetables or to store for later use.

Dill Marinade
(great for marinating raw vegetables)

Makes 2 cups

¾ cup vegetable oil
¼ cup olive oil
1 cup wine vinegar
1 tablespoon granulated sugar
1 tablespoon chopped dried dill weed
1 teaspoon black pepper
Dash of garlic powder

1. Place all the ingredients in a tightly covered container. Shake to blend well.

2. Store the marinade on a kitchen shelf or in the refrigerator. Shake well and have at room temperature before using.

Yogurt-Mint Marinade
(especially good over cucumbers)

Makes 1⅓ cups

1 cup plain yogurt
¼ cup chopped fresh mint
1 tablespoon lemon juice
1 tablespoon chopped fresh chives
1 teaspoon honey
½ teaspoon salt

1. Combine all the ingredients in a bowl.

2. Keep refrigerated until ready to use.

Miso Dressing and Marinade
(a salad dressing or vegetable marinade)

Makes 1 cup

½ cup vegetable oil
¼ cup water
2 tablespoons rice vinegar or lemon juice
2 tablespoons miso
1 tablespoon honey
Juice from 1 clove garlic
Dash of dry mustard
1 teaspoon chopped fresh chives
½ teaspoon tahini or sesame seeds (optional)

1. Combine all the ingredients in a blender and mix well.

2. Refrigerate until ready to use.

Note: This is also delicious when heated and used to sauté mushrooms, zucchini, or other vegetables.

SALAD DRESSINGS

Black French Dressing   Makes 1½ cups

¼ cup wine vinegar or lemon juice
¾ cup vegetable oil
¼ teaspoon black pepper
1 tablespoon molasses
½ cup finely chopped black olives

1. Combine all the ingredients in a tightly covered container. Shake well to blend.

2. Store the dressing in the refrigerator but bring it to room temperature before serving.

Blue Cheese Dressing   Makes 2⅓ cups

1 cup mayonnaise
½ cup crumbled blue cheese
½ cup sour cream or plain yogurt
⅓ cup milk
1 tablespoon granulated sugar
2 tablespoons distilled white vinegar
1 teaspoon Worcestershire sauce
⅛ teaspoon black pepper
Juice from 1 clove garlic

1. Combine all the ingredients.

2. Store, covered, in the refrigerator. If the dressing thickens upon standing, thin it with milk.

Italian Dressing   Makes 1¼ cups

¾ cup vegetable oil
¼ cup olive oil
2 tablespoons Italian Seasoning (page 48)
¼ cup red wine vinegar
Juice from 1 clove garlic
Dash of Salad Herbs (page 49)

1. Combine all the ingredients in a container with a tight-fitting top. Shake well and store in a kitchen cabinet or in a refrigerator.

2. When ready to use, shake well. The dressing should be served at room temperature for best flavor.

Note: This can be served over the traditional tossed salad or a combination of tomato wedges and sliced Bermuda onions.

Peanut Butter Dressing
(for a fruit salad)

Makes 1½ cups

¼ cup peanut butter
1 cup mayonnaise
⅓ cup honey
¾ cup light cream

1 tablespoon dry white wine
1½ tablespoons lemon juice
4 ounces cream cheese

1. Mix the ingredients together in a blender. If too thick, add additional cream until the dressing is the desired consistency.

2. Refrigerate until ready to use.

SAUCES

Barbecue Sauce   Makes 1¾ cups

½ cup cider vinegar
1 tablespoon Chili Powder (page 50)
    or Curry Powder (page 48)
Juice from 1 clove garlic

1 teaspoon Salad Herbs (page 49)
¼ cup tomato paste
1 cup Vegetable Stock (page 76)

1. Combine all the ingredients in a saucepan and cook over low heat until the sauce is thick.

2. Store the sauce in a tightly covered jar in the refrigerator.

Spaghetti Sauce   Makes 3¾ cups

2 tablespoons vegetable oil
2 tablespoons Italian Seasoning (page 48)
Juice from 1 clove garlic
1 teaspoon anchovy paste (optional)
1 medium onion, finely chopped
1 tablespoon granulated sugar
1 can (6 ounces) tomato paste
1 can (28 ounces) plum tomatoes, with liquid
1 can (8 ounces) mushroom pieces, with liquid

1. In a heavy saucepan, heat the oil. Add the spices, anchovy paste, and onion. Sauté the mixture for 5 minutes.

2. Add the remaining ingredients, mixing well to break up the tomatoes. Simmer, covered, for as long as you have the time; the longer the better. Stir often to keep from burning on the bottom. If the sauce is too thin, cook without a lid to allow for evaporation. If it is too thick, add a little water.

3. Place sauce in a container and refrigerate until ready to use.

Uncooked Tomato Sauce   Makes 2 cups

2 cans (1 pound) plum tomatoes, drained and finely chopped
1 medium onion, minced
2 scallions, thinly sliced
Juice from 1 clove garlic
Salt
1 tablespoon dried tarragon or ground coriander
1 teaspoon granulated sugar
Dash of Tabasco sauce

1. Combine all the ingredients in a mixing bowl and blend well.

2. Purée the mixture if a smoother consistency is desired; otherwise, simply use as is.

Pesto Sauce   Makes 1½ cups

2 teaspoons chopped fresh basil
½ cup chopped fresh parsley
½ cup grated Parmesan cheese
⅓ cup chopped pine nuts or walnuts
Juice from 1 clove garlic
¼ to ½ cup olive oil

1. Place the basil, parsley, cheese, nuts, and garlic juice in a blender and purée, adding oil as needed to arrive at a soft paste.

2. Put the paste in a container until ready to use.

Harissa Sauce   Makes ¼ cup

3 tablespoons Conserie D'Harissa (page 50)
¼ cup olive oil
2 tablespoons lemon juice
Juice from 1 clove garlic

1. Combine all the ingredients in a saucepan and cook over low heat, stirring constantly, for about 5 minutes. Thin with additional lemon juice and olive oil if desired.

2. Place the sauce in a tightly covered container in the refrigerator until ready to use.

Chinese Hot Mustard Sauce

Makes 1 serving

1 tablespoon dry mustard   Stale beer
Pinch of turmeric

1. Mix the dry mustard with the turmeric and enough stale beer to make a thin paste.

2. Use in contrast to sweet or mild foods. It is especially good for dipping foods, but remember that it is very hot!

Peanut Sauce

Makes 1 cup

¼ cup vegetable oil
½ cup shelled raw peanuts
½ cup Spicy Soy Sauce (page 72)
¼ cup lemon juice
Juice from 1 clove garlic

1. Heat the oil in a skillet or wok. Stir-fry the peanuts until they are golden. Drain on paper toweling.

2. Grind the peanuts in a blender, then combine with the remaining ingredients.

3. Serve either hot or at room temperature. Refrigerate for storage.

Spicy Soy Sauce   Makes 1¾ cups

¼ cup rice vinegar
3 tablespoons Conserie D'Harissa (page 50)
2 tablespoons peeled and grated gingerroot
1 cup soy sauce
½ cup sesame oil

1. Combine all the ingredients in a tightly covered jar. Shake well.

2. Chill until ready to serve. This sauce will keep almost indefinitely.

Sweet and Sour Sauce   Makes 1⅓ cups

½ cup honey
½ cup orange juice
⅓ cup cider vinegar
1 tablespoon dry mustard
1 tablespoon turmeric
1 teaspoon ground ginger
1 teaspoon arrowroot
1 tablespoon cold water

1. Combine the honey and orange juice in a saucepan. Simmer until the
liquid is reduced slightly in volume.

2. Add the vinegar, mustard, turmeric, and ginger and continue to simmer.

3. Combine the arrowroot and water in a small bowl and make a paste. Stir the paste into the sauce, then cook the sauce, stirring constantly, until it has thickened.

4. Use immediately, in Chinese-style dishes or over a wedge of steamed cabbage.

Cheese Yogurt Sauce   Makes 1½ cups

1 cup plain yogurt
1 tablespoon all-purpose flour
1 tablespoon prepared mustard

1 cup grated sharp cheddar cheese
Milk or stale beer

1. Place the yogurt, flour, and mustard in a blender and purée.

2. Pour the yogurt mixture into a saucepan and add the cheese. Cook over low heat, stirring constantly, until the cheese is melted and the sauce is hot. Add the milk or beer as needed to arrive at the desired consistency.

Lemon Yogurt Sauce I   Makes 1 cup
(for a cold sauce)

1 large egg   2 to 4 tablespoons lemon juice
½ teaspoon dry mustard   1 cup plain yogurt

1. In a blender, combine the egg, mustard, and lemon juice with ¼ cup of the yogurt. Blend on low speed.

2. Uncover the blender and slowly add the remaining yogurt as the blender continues to run.

3. Refrigerate until ready to use.

Lemon Yogurt Sauce II   Makes 1 cup
(for a hot sauce)

1 cup plain yogurt   1 teaspoon mayonnaise (optional)
1 tablespoon all-purpose flour   2 to 4 tablespoons lemon juice

1. Combine the ingredients in a bowl and mix well.

2. Refrigerate until ready to use in a recipe.

STOCKS

Since vegetables are the mainstay of a vegetarian diet, it is important to make optimum use of them. Reserve a large covered container in your refrigerator for the collection of liquids drained off canned or cooked vegetables. Before you know it, you will have a flavorful stock — useful in a dozen different ways. In addition to making your own economical and delicious stock, you will also have the advantage of being able to reduce the fat in the stock. Once the liquids are thoroughly chilled, any fat that is in it will float to the top and become solid; simply lift it off. Your stock should be heated to a rolling boil every few days to keep it fresh. Rechill it immediately.

Chinese Broth   Makes 4 to 6 cups

1 cup soybean sprouts   Soy sauce
4 to 6 cups water   White pepper
Few drops Preheated Oil (page 51)

1. Combine the sprouts and water in a large pot. Bring to a boil and then simmer for 1 hour.

2. Remove the pot from the heat and season to taste with oil, soy sauce, pepper. Reserve the broth for use in soups or in cooking.

Note: Do not use unsprouted soybeans; the flavor of the broth will be unpleasantly strong.

Vegetable Stock   Makes 2 quarts

2 quarts water
4 cups chopped onions
2 cups chopped carrots
1 large potato, chopped and with peel
⅔ cups chopped celery with tops
3 medium tomatoes, chopped
1 tablespoon chopped fresh parsley
1 teaspoon dried thyme leaves
1 teaspoon chopped dried basil
1 clove garlic, chopped
Salt and black pepper

1. Combine all the ingredients and simmer, covered, for 1 hour.

2. Strain the stock through a fine sieve or cheesecloth before using. Discard the solids.

Note: For a clearer stock, omit the potato but still add the peel.

5

Rice and Other Tasty Grains

RICE AND OTHER TASTY GRAINS

We use the seeds of various cereal grasses in our everyday cooking, almost without thinking about them. The most common grain is rice, but we also use wheat, oats, and rye in their various forms. Usually these grains are served as side dishes, along with meat. However, in the vegetarian kitchen, the grains very often become the central part of the meal.

RICE

Rice is the staple in many countries of the world, where brown rice is widely used. In the United States, white rice is still preferred, although more and more people in the supermarkets are picking up packages of brown rice instead. Rice that is white has had the hull removed, then the bran surrounding the kernel is milled away. Brown rice has that layer of bran still on it, thus providing roughage, as well as thiamin, niacin, and iron. In the recipes that follow, we use a combination of brown and white rice, depending upon the individual recipe. Wild rice also appears in the recipes, and this is from a different grass from regular rice. It is considered a delicacy and is usually used in small quantities.

To cook white rice, measure 1 part the amount of rice you need and place in a saucepan. Add 2 to 3 parts water and a pinch of salt. Bring rice to a boil, cover, and simmer for about 20 minutes, or until rice is done. To cook brown rice, allow additional cooking time — up to 45 minutes.

Brown Rice and Carrot Soup   Serves 4

5 cups Vegetable Stock (page 76)
¼ cup raw long-grain brown rice
¼ teaspoon dried marjoram
½ teaspoon chopped dried dill weed
1½ cups peeled and diced carrots
¼ cup chopped fresh parsley
⅛ teaspoon black pepper
1 tablespoon lemon juice

1. Bring 2 cups of stock to a boil and add the rice. Cover and simmer for 30 minutes.

2. Add the remaining stock and the remaining ingredients except the lemon juice. Bring to a boil, cover, and simmer until the carrots are tender — about 5 minutes.

3. Remove from the heat and stir in the lemon juice. Serve.

Brown Rice Burgers

Serves 4 to 6

3 tablespoons vegetable oil
1 large onion, finely chopped
1 cup finely chopped celery
½ cup chopped fresh parsley
Juice from 1 clove garlic
4 cups cooked brown rice
2 cups peeled and coarsely grated carrots
2 large eggs, lightly beaten
½ cup whole-wheat flour
Black pepper
Vegetable oil for frying

1. In a large skillet, heat the oil and combine the next 4 ingredients. Sauté for 10 minutes.

2. Place the rice, carrots, eggs, flour, and pepper in a bowl and add the cooked ingredients. Blend and shape into patties, adding more flour if the patties are too soft to hold their shape.

3. Heat the oil and fry the patties over medium heat until they are browned on both sides. Serve with Cheese Yogurt Sauce (page 73) or Lemon Yogurt Sauce (page 74).

Mexican Brown Rice   Serves 5 to 6

2 cups Vegetable Stock (page 76)
1 large onion, chopped
1 large tomato, peeled and seeded
Juice from 1 clove garlic
3 tablespoons vegetable oil
2 cups raw brown rice

1. Combine ½ cup of stock with the onion, tomato, and garlic juice in a
    blender. Mix until well blended.

2. Heat the oil in a large skillet over medium to high heat. Add the rice
    and sauté for 6 to 8 minutes.

3. Stir in the tomato mixture and the remaining stock. Bring to a boil,
    then reduce the heat, cover, and simmer until the liquid is absorbed
    — about 45 minutes.

4. Fluff the rice with a fork and serve immediately.

Mushroom-Rice Casserole   Serves 8

2 tablespoons vegetable oil
½ pound fresh mushrooms, stems removed and chopped, caps left whole
1 medium onion, minced
1 tablespoon Curry Powder (page 48)
2 medium apples, chopped fine
2 teaspoons paprika
Black pepper
2⅔ cups plain yogurt
2 cups cooked brown rice

1. Preheat the oven to 350 degrees.

2. Heat the oil in a skillet. Sauté the mushroom caps in the oil, then remove from the pan and set aside.

3. In the same skillet, sauté the onion and the curry powder until the onion is wilted.

4. Add the chopped apples and the reserved chopped mushroom stems and sauté for 5 minutes. Remove from the heat and stir in the paprika, pepper, and yogurt.

5. Place the cooked rice in a buttered 2-quart casserole. Pour the mushroom-yogurt sauce over the rice. Arrange the mushroom caps on top, and sprinkle with additional paprika if desired.

6. Bake for 45 minutes, then serve.

Nutty Wild Rice Ring

Serves 6 to 8

8 large stalks celery, finely chopped
1 cup cooked wild rice
¾ cup ground pecans
⅓ cup finely minced onion
⅓ cup finely minced green pepper
2 tablespoons chopped fresh parsley
1 tablespoon all-purpose flour
3 large eggs, lightly beaten
1½ cups milk
3 tablespoons butter, melted
½ teaspoon black pepper

1. Preheat the oven to 350 degrees.

2. In a mixing bowl, combine the celery, rice, pecans, onion, green pepper, parsley, and flour. Mix well.

3. In another bowl, combine the eggs, milk, butter, and pepper. Stir this into the rice mixture.

4. Pour the mixture into a well-buttered 1¼-quart ring mold. Set the mold in a hot-water bath and bake for 1 hour or until set.

5. Remove the mold from the water, let it stand for 15 minutes, then unmold it onto a heated serving platter. Fill with a vegetable of contrasting color if desired.

Pilaf

Serves 6 to 8

2 cups Vegetable Stock (page 76)
2 tablespoons vegetable oil
1 tablespoon Middle Eastern Spice (page 47) or Conserie D'Harissa
    (page 50)
Handful of raw thin egg noodles
1 cup raw long-grain rice

1. Bring the stock to a boil and keep it hot.

2. In a heavy pan, heat the oil over medium to high heat, then add the spices. Add the noodles, stirring constantly to coat them with the spices and to brown them without burning.

3. Add the rice to the pan and stir to coat with the spices. Slowly add the hot liquid, being careful not to splatter. Stir, cover, and reduce the heat to low. Simmer the rice until the liquid is absorbed — about 25 minutes.

Rice Pilaf with Bulgur   Serves 6

2 cups Vegetable Stock (page 76)
¼ cup butter
1 medium onion, chopped
¾ cup raw long-grain rice
¼ cup raw bulgur
Salt and black pepper
½ cup raisins
¼ cup pine nuts
¼ cup fresh or frozen peas, cooked briefly (optional)

1. Heat the stock until very hot. Keep warm.

2. Melt the butter over medium heat in a heavy saucepan. Add the onion and sauté it for 5 minutes.

3. Add the rice and continue to sauté, stirring until the rice is golden. Add the hot stock, bulgur, salt, and pepper.

4. Reduce the heat, cover the pan, and simmer until all the liquid is absorbed — about 25 minutes.

5. Remove the pan from the heat, add the remaining ingredients, recover pan, and let stand to heat through. Serve.

Wild Rice Salad   Serves 6

⅓ cup vegetable oil
2 cups raw wild rice
4 cups Vegetable Stock (page 76)
1 cup French dressing (any commercial variety or your own blend)
⅔ cup thinly sliced water chestnuts
½ cup very thinly sliced sweet red pepper
¼ cup minced shallots or scallions
Black pepper
¾ pound snow peas, tips and strings removed
½ pound fresh mushrooms, thinly sliced

1. In a heavy casserole, heat the oil over moderate heat. Add the rice and sauté for about 5 minutes, or until the rice begins to darken; stir often.

2. Stir in the vegetable stock, cover the pan, and reduce the heat to low. Simmer until the liquid is absorbed — about 1 hour.

3. When the rice is cooked, toss it while still warm with ¼ cup dressing. Let the rice mixture cool.

4. Add the water chestnuts, red pepper, shallots, and pepper to the rice, then add another ¼ cup dressing and toss. Chill for 1 hour.

5. Meanwhile, cover the snow peas with boiling water. Let them stand for 1 minute, then drain. Rinse with cold water and pat dry. Cut the snow peas into 1-inch pieces and toss them with ¼ cup dressing.

6. Combine the mushrooms and the remaining dressing. Add them to the snow peas and toss to mix.

7. To serve, either mix the rice and the snow pea-mushroom mixtures together or transfer the rice to a large serving bowl, make a well in the center, and mound the snow pea-mushroom mixture in the well.

Sesame Tomatoes on Rice   Serves 6

¼ cup vegetable oil
1½ cups chopped onion
2 cups raw brown rice
4 cups Vegetable Stock (page 76)
1 teaspoon Italian Seasoning (page 48)
Juice from 1 clove garlic
12 firm tomato slices, cut ½ inch thick
2 large eggs, beaten
½ cup sesame seeds
Vegetable oil for frying
Grated Parmesan cheese

1. In a large saucepan, heat the oil, then add the onion and rice and sauté until they are coated with oil and are golden.

2. Add the stock and the seasonings. Cover and simmer until the liquid is absorbed — about 1 hour.

3. Meanwhile, dip the tomato slices in the beaten egg and then in the sesame seeds, coating both sides. Fry the slices in hot oil, browning the outsides. Do not overcook — you don't want them mushy, so cook them quickly over high heat. Remove the tomatoes from the pan as soon as they are brown and drain on a paper towel.

4. To serve, arrange the rice on a platter, cover with sesame-coated tomatoes, and sprinkle with Parmesan cheese.

BARLEY, BULGUR, AND BUCKWHEAT

There are other grains besides rice that can be used for variety in your meals. Barley is best known for its use in soups but it can be enjoyed also in other ways. It is sold most commonly as pearled barley (bran removed and kernel polished).

Bulgur is wheat that has gone through a series of processes, including the removal of the bran. It is becoming more popular in this country, although it has been a staple in the Middle East for centuries.

Buckwheat comes from a herbaceous plant rather than a grass. The seeds are ground into flour or used as a cereal, referred to as buckwheat groats. When the groats are toasted, they are called kasha.

Grains such as these require no presoaking, although they should be rinsed. They cook in about 1 hour or less time, and will expand in volume about threefold.

To cook grains, first heat approximately ¼ cup of butter or vegetable oil per cup of grain. Add seasonings of your choice, then stir in the grains, coating the kernels with the oil-spice mixture. Add hot water or broth, stir gently, cover the pan, and reduce the heat to low. Cook until the grains are of desired tenderness and moisture. Add additional liquid if needed, but be careful not to drown the grains or they will become mushy.

Cooked grains can be stored in the refrigerator for about 1 week, but they don't keep well in the freezer.

Barley Mushroom Soup   Serves 4

¼ cup raw barley
3 cups Vegetable Stock (page 76)
2 tablespoons butter
1 pound fresh mushrooms, sliced
1 small onion, thinly sliced
Black pepper

1. Simmer the barley, covered, in the stock until tender — about 1 hour.

2. Melt the butter in a skillet and sauté the mushrooms and onion.

3. Purée half the mushroom-onion mixture in a blender, along with the pepper and enough stock to allow for a thorough blending.

4. Stir the puréed mixture, as well as the remaining mushrooms and onions, into the barley mixture. Heat thoroughly and serve.

Barley Pilaf

Serves 6 to 8

¼ cup butter
1 medium onion, finely chopped
½ pound fresh mushrooms, thinly sliced
1 cup raw barley
2 teaspoons Middle Eastern Spice (page 47)
3 cups hot Vegetable Stock (page 76)

1. In a large saucepan, melt the butter and add the onion and mushrooms. Sauté for 5 minutes.

2. Stir in the barley and the spice, mixing thoroughly. Add the hot stock, cover, and cook over low heat until the barley is tender — about 1 hour. Serve.

Bulgur Seed Loaf

Serves 6

1 cup softened bulgur
1 cup cooked soy grits
⅓ cup coarsely ground sesame or sunflower seeds
1⅔ cups bread crumbs
2 large eggs, lightly beaten
1 to 2 cups tomato sauce, as needed
2 cups chopped leftover vegetables
Black pepper

1. Preheat the oven to 350 degrees.

2. Combine all the ingredients in a large mixing bowl, reserving ½ cup of tomato sauce for the topping.

3. Pour the mixture into a greased loaf pan and bake for 1 hour. Let the loaf stand about 15 minutes before slicing. Top with tomato sauce.

Basic Kasha

Serves 4

1 cup whole kasha
1 large egg
1 tablespoon vegetable oil

4 cups water or stock
1 teaspoon salt

1. In a mixing bowl, combine the kasha and the egg. Mix thoroughly.

2. Heat the oil in a saucepan and add the kasha. Cook, stirring, over medium heat until the grains are separated.

3. Add the water and the salt and bring the liquid to a boil. Cover, reduce the heat to low, and cook until the liquid is absorbed — about 20 minutes.

4. Serve as a side dish. For a special treat, stir cooked kasha into cubed and steamed winter squash.

Kasha Balls

Serves 4

1½ cups Basic Kasha (see previous recipe)
1 cup peeled and shredded eggplant
¼ cup minced onion
¼ cup diced green pepper
2 large eggs, lightly beaten
Juice from 1 clove garlic
1 teaspoon Italian Seasoning (page 48)
Salt and black pepper
2 tablespoons all-purpose flour

1. Preheat the oven to 375 degrees.

2. In a large mixing bowl, combine all the ingredients. Mix thoroughly. Add more flour if necessary to bind ingredients.

3. Form 12 balls and place them in an oiled baking pan. Bake the balls for 30 minutes, then place them under the broiler for several minutes to brown.

4. Serve the balls with a cheese or tomato sauce.

Barley-Vegetable Stew   Serves 6

¼ cup vegetable oil
1 medium eggplant, peeled and cut into 1-inch cubes
2 medium zucchini, cut into ¼-inch slices
2 carrots, peeled and cut into ¼-inch slices
1½ cups chopped onions
1 can (1-pound) whole tomatoes with juice
¾ cup raw barley
1½ cups Vegetable Stock (page 76)
1 teaspoon dried oregano
Black pepper
Juice from 1 clove garlic
2 cups grated cheddar cheese

1. Preheat the oven to 350 degrees.

2. In a large, heavy casserole, heat the vegetable oil. Add the fresh vegetables and sauté for 5 minutes over medium heat.

3. Add the tomatoes, barley, stock, and seasonings, stirring to break the tomatoes into pieces.

4. Remove the casserole from the heat and add 1 cup of the cheese. Stir until well blended. Cover the casserole and bake in the oven for 45 minutes.

5. Sprinkle the stew with the remaining cheese but do not stir it in. Continue to bake, uncovered, for 15 minutes more. Serve.

Tabbouleh   Serves 8

1 cup raw bulgur
1¾ cups water or stock
½ cup lemon juice
Juice from 1 clove garlic
1 cup finely chopped onion
1 cup finely chopped fresh parsley
½ cup finely chopped fresh mint
Black pepper
1 cup chopped fresh tomatoes
⅓ cup olive oil

1. In a mixing bowl, combine the bulgur, water, ¼ cup of lemon juice, and garlic juice. Set aside to allow the bulgur to soften — about 30 minutes for refined bulgur, 1 hour for unrefined bulgur. When the bulgur is soft, drain off any unabsorbed liquid, pressing out excess.

2. In a large bowl, combine the bulgur with the remaining ingredients, including the remaining lemon juice. Toss well and chill before serving.

Sweet Couscous

Barley Salad   Serves 6

2½ cups raw barley
7½ cups Vegetable Stock (page 76)
3 tablespoons lemon juice
½ cup olive oil
1 large cucumber, finely chopped
¾ cup thinly sliced radishes
¾ cup chopped fresh parsley
⅓ cup thinly sliced scallions
Black pepper

1. Cook the barley in the stock until the liquid is absorbed — about 1 hour.

2. Combine the lemon juice and oil, then add to the hot barley and toss well.

3. Add the remaining ingredients and chill before serving.

Barley with Butter and Cheese Serves 1

3 tablespoons butter
1 cup cooked barley
2 tablespoons grated Parmesan and/or Romano cheese

1. Melt the butter in a skillet and add the barley. Stir to heat thoroughly; add a little water or stock if the mixture is too dry or sticky.

2. Sprinkle the barley with the cheese.

3. Serve while the mixture is hot.

Note: This is something for late at night when you are craving a little something different.

CORN (GRITS)

We all know corn as a vegetable, but it also is a grain, providing us with hominy grits. The kernels of corn are hulled and dried, then sold as hominy, but when the hominy is ground, we get the grits. Try the following recipes, one being a traditional use of grits, the other a little different.

Hominy Grits with Egg   Serves 1

1 individual-size package instant grits
½ cup boiling water
1 teaspoon butter
1 large egg

1. Preheat the oven to 350 degrees.

2. Combine the grits with the water in a small baking dish.

3. Top the grits with the butter and then the egg. Cover the dish with a small piece of foil and bake until the egg is cooked to your preference. Serve for a hearty breakfast.

Hominy Grits Ring   Serves 6

5 cups water
1½ teaspoons salt
1¼ cups quick-cooking hominy grits
4 to 5 scallions, chopped fine, including greens
⅓ cup finely chopped fresh parsley
1 large egg, lightly beaten
1 tablespoon butter, melted
¼ cup bread crumbs
¼ cup grated Parmesan cheese
1 cup tomato sauce

1. Bring the water to a boil and add the salt. Stir in the grits and reduce the heat to medium. Cook, covered, for 30 minutes.

2. Add the scallions and parsley to the grits, then spoon the mixture into a lightly oiled 1½-quart ring mold. Allow it to stand for 30 minutes.

3. Preheat the oven to 375 degrees.

4. Beat together the egg and butter. Unmold the ring mold and brush the grits with the egg-butter mixture.

5. Combine the bread crumbs and the cheese, then dust the mold with this mixture. Replace the grits ring in the mold and bake until golden — about 10 minutes. Unmold and serve with heated tomato sauce.

SOME OTHER ITEMS

There are some other food items that should be considered along with the grains in this chapter. One is bran, that substance we now look to so much for more fiber in our diets. Bran is the outer layer of grains, often removed in the milling process. Most often it is used in breakfast cereals or in desserts. I have given you some recipes for bran in the baking chapter (page 289).

Another grain to be considered is oats. We are most familiar with rolled oats, which are flakes sold commonly as oatmeal. Granola is also made from rolled oats, and this is a tasty combination of toasted grains and ground seeds. To this mixture is added nuts, raisins, and so forth. I have included a recipe for granola on page 281.

Wheat germ is the embryo in the grain, from which a new plant would develop if the seed were allowed to grow. When flour is milled, the germ is separated from the rest of the kernel, although it is returned to the whole-wheat flour. You will find a recipe for Wheat Germ-Cheese Bars in the Bread, Biscuits, and Other Baked Goods chapter, but in this section we include a recipe for a salad using wheat germ.

Lastly, we have couscous, which is a type of cereal from semolina wheat. I include 2 recipes for this.

High Fiber Slaw

Serves 4 to 6

1 small head cabbage, shredded
⅔ cup toasted wheat germ
¼ cup chopped green onions or scallions
⅓ cup minced fresh parsley
½ cup chopped almonds
1 cup plain yogurt
½ teaspoon chopped fresh dill
¼ teaspoon dry mustard

1. Combine the first 5 ingredients in a large mixing bowl.

2. In a small bowl, mix together the yogurt, dill, and mustard as a dressing.

3. Pour the dressing over the slaw and toss to coat well. Chill before serving.

Basic Couscous

Makes 6 cups

1 package (16 ounces) precooked couscous
½ cup cold water
1½ cups warm water
¼ teaspoon ground saffron or turmeric

1. To cook couscous, ideally you need a couscousiere or a large steamer. If you don't have either, then locate a pan that is wide enough to let a colander nestle on top and that is deep enough to be partially filled with water without the water touching the colander. The top and bottom pans will need to be tightly sealed at the sides to allow steam from the boiling water in the bottom to cook the couscous through the holes in the top. If the pans do not form a tight seal, dampen a length of cheesecloth, twist it tightly, and fit it into the space between the pans.

2. Combine the couscous with the cold water in a large bowl, in order to moisten the grains.

3. Transfer the couscous to the top pan, placed over boiling water. If the holes in the colander are so large as to allow the couscous to slip through, just line the colander with cheesecloth. Steam the couscous, uncovered for 15 minutes.

4. Transfer the couscous back to the large bowl. Add ½ cup warm water and rub the couscous between your fingers until all the grains are separated. Place the couscous back in the top pan and steam, uncovered, for 15 more minutes.

5. Repeat step 4.

6. Repeat step 4 again, using ½ cup of warm water, but this time add the saffron or turmeric to the water. After this last 15 minutes of steaming, the couscous should be tender and ready to eat or to use in another recipe.

Sweet Couscous   Serves 4

2 cups dark raisins
4 large onions, sliced
2 cups water
½ cup Vegetable Stock (page 76)
1 cup honey
1 teaspoon ground cinnamon
¼ teaspoon ground saffron or turmeric

1 tablespoon butter, melted
½ teaspoon salt
6 cups Basic Couscous (page 102)
1 small zucchini, parboiled
 and thinly sliced

1. Soak the raisins in cold water to cover for 30 minutes. Drain.

2. Combine the onions with the 2 cups of water in a saucepan. Simmer, covered, until the onions are translucent — about 30 to 40 minutes.

3. Add the raisins to the onions and bring the mixture to a boil. Cook, uncovered and liquid boiling, until the liquid has all evaporated — about 5 minutes.

4. Add the stock, honey, and spices and simmer, uncovered, until the mixture is thick — about 20 minutes.

5. Stir the butter and salt into the steamed couscous.

6. Place the couscous in a serving dish and pour the onion-raisin mixture over it. Decorate platter with thin slices of zucchini. Serve.

CHAPTER

6

Vegetables — The Wonders of the Garden

VEGETABLES – THE WONDERS OF THE GARDEN

I used to think of vegetables as fillers — mere accompaniments to meat. But no more! These vegetable recipes don't need to take a back seat; they're stars in their own right.

ASPARAGUS

Asparagus Chinese-Style   Serves 4

2 tablespoons vegetable oil
2 teaspoons fermented black
  beans, mashed
Dash of garlic powder
1 tablespoon Spicy Soy Sauce (page 72)

2 teaspoons granulated sugar
1 pound fresh asparagus,
  cut into slices or strips
1 teaspoon sesame oil

1. Combine the first 5 ingredients in a skillet or wok and place over high heat.

2. Add the asparagus and sauté, adding a spoonful or two of water to create steam to cook the vegetables. Stir constantly but gently until the asparagus is cooked — about 5 minutes.

3. Just before serving, toss with sesame oil.

Asparagus-Potato Salad   Serves 6

2 pounds small red-skinned potatoes, unpeeled
1½ cups Dill Marinade (page 63)
1 tablespoon dry mustard
2 pounds fresh asparagus, cooked tender-crisp
Hard-boiled eggs, sliced or quartered (optional)

1. Cook the potatoes until just tender, then allow to cool. Slice in ¼-inch pieces.

2. Combine the dill marinade with the mustard. Pour this over the potatoes, cover, and refrigerate overnight.

3. Arrange the cooked asparagus on a large platter. Remove the potatoes from the marinade with a slotted spoon and mound them attractively on top of the asparagus. Add the pieces of hard-boiled egg, then pour the marinade over all and serve.

Batter-Fried Asparagus   Serves 4

24 fresh asparagus spears
1½ cups all-purpose flour
½ teaspoon baking powder
Salt and black pepper
¾ cup finely grated gruyère cheese
½ teaspoon grated lemon rind
1¼ cups milk
1 large egg
Dash of Worcestershire sauce
Vegetable oil for deep-frying
Lemon wedges

1. Cut the asparagus at about 1½ inches below the tips. Reserve the tender parts of the stems for soups or the stock pot.

2. Bring salted water to a boil in a small saucepan and cook the tips for 1 minute. Drain and pat dry.

3. In a mixing bowl, combine the flour, baking powder, seasonings, cheese, and lemon rind. Blend well.

4. In a separate bowl, beat together the milk, egg, and Worcestershire sauce, then slowly stir this into the dry mixture. Blend completely and let stand for 30 minutes at room temperature or covered and refrigerated for up to 2 hours. If the mixture becomes too thick, thin with a small amount of milk. The mixture should be the consistency of sour cream.

5. Heat the oil to 375 degrees. Using a long-handled fork, dip each asparagus tip into the batter and then drop it into the heated oil. Fry until each side is puffed and golden — it should take only a few seconds. Remove with a slotted spoon and drain well. Serve with lemon wedges.

Note: Asparagus may be frozen after cooking if desired. To reheat, place on a baking sheet and bake in a preheated 400-degree oven for 10 to 12 minutes.

BEETS

Beets and Cucumbers in Cream   Serves 4 to 6

4 to 5 fresh medium beets
2 large cucumbers, peeled, seeded, and cut into ½-inch slices
1 tablespoon white wine vinegar
Salt
4 tablespoons butter
Black pepper
1 cup heavy (whipping) cream
2 tablespoons sour cream
3 tablespoons minced fresh chives
Lemon juice

1. In a large saucepan, cover the beets with water and bring to a boil. Simmer until tender — about 1 hour. Drain, allow to cool, then peel and cube. Set aside.

2. Place the cucumber slices in a colander. Sprinkle with vinegar and salt and let stand 1 hour to drain.

3. Melt 2 tablespoons of butter in a large, heavy skillet over medium heat. Add the cucumbers and sauté until they are lightly browned — about 4 minutes. Remove the cucumbers with a slotted spoon and set aside.

4. Reduce the heat to low and add the remaining butter, the beets, and pepper. Cook for 4 minutes.

5. Stir in the heavy cream and bring to a boil. Cook until the cream is reduced to a thick sauce. Be careful that the sauce does not burn.

6. Add the cucumbers, sour cream, and chives and cook for 4 minutes, then add the lemon juice and additional pepper to taste. Serve hot or cold.

Beets in Sour Cream   Serves 4

2 cups peeled and diced raw beets
½ cup chopped onion
⅛ teaspoon caraway seeds
1 cup water
½ cup sour cream
2 teaspoons white distilled vinegar
½ teaspoon prepared horseradish

1. Combine the beets, onion, caraway seeds, and water in a saucepan. Cover tightly, bring to a boil, then simmer until the beets are tender — about 15 minutes.

2. Combine the remaining ingredients and add to the beets. Serve hot.

Grated Beets with Orange   Serves 4

4 large raw beets, peeled and grated
¾ cup orange juice
15 to 20 drops bitters

1. Combine all the ingredients in a saucepan.

2. Bring to a boil, then simmer for 5 minutes; the beets should be
slightly crisp. Serve hot.

BROCCOLI

Cream of Broccoli Soup   Serves 6

2 tablespoons butter
1 cup minced onion
½ cup thinly sliced celery
1½ pounds fresh broccoli
6 cups Vegetable Stock (page 76)

2 cups light cream
Salt and black pepper
Juice from 1 clove garlic
Chopped fresh parsley

1. In a heavy soup pot, heat the butter, then add the onion and celery.
Sauté until the vegetables are tender.

2. Separate the broccoli into flowerets and stalks. Cut the stalks into small pieces, and reserve the flowerets. Add the stalks and the stock to the onion mixture. Simmer 15 minutes, then add the flowerets and simmer another 15 minutes.

3. Purée the mixture in a blender, then return the purée to the pot. Stir in the cream and seasonings and heat gently.

4. Serve hot, garnished with parsley.

Broccoli Fritters   Serves 6 to 8

1 large egg
1 cup milk
2 cups all-purpose flour
2 teaspoons baking powder

¾ teaspoon salt
1½ cups chopped fresh broccoli
Vegetable oil for deep-frying

1. Combine all the ingredients except the oil in a blender. Run the machine and blend the ingredients until the broccoli is finely chopped but not puréed.

2. Heat the oil to 375 degrees. Drop the batter by tablespoons into the hot oil and cook until golden brown — about 4 minutes.

3. Drain the cooked fritters on paper towels and serve with Cheese Yogurt Sauce (page 73).

Broccoli and Rice Casserole   Serves 8

10 tablespoons butter
¾ cup finely chopped onion
¾ cup chopped fresh mushrooms
½ cup all-purpose flour
3 cups Vegetable Stock (page 76)
2 packages (10 ounces) frozen chopped broccoli, cooked until tender-crisp

1 cup evaporated milk
Black pepper
½ cup bread crumbs
2½ cups cooked rice

1. Preheat the oven to 350 degrees.

2. Heat ½ cup of butter in a large pan and sauté the onion and mushrooms.

3. Stir in the flour, mixing well. Add the stock, milk, and pepper and cook until the sauce comes to a boil. Remove from the heat and set aside.

4. In a small skillet, heat the remaining butter and brown the bread crumbs.

5. Place the rice in a buttered 2½-quart casserole. Top with the broccoli, then the sauce. Sprinkle the bread crumbs over the top.

6. Bake the casserole uncovered until the sauce bubbles — about 30 minutes. Serve hot.

CABBAGE

Hot Slaw   Serves 6

¼ cup Vegetable Stock (page 76)
5 cups shredded green cabbage
1 cup shredded carrots
½ cup chopped green onion or scallions
½ teaspoon black pepper
¼ cup butter
1 teaspoon prepared mustard
⅓ cup chopped pecans
¼ teaspoon paprika

1. In a heavy saucepan, bring the stock to a boil. Add the cabbage, carrots, onion, and pepper. Cover and cook over low heat for 5 minutes, stirring occasionally. Drain and set aside.

2. Melt the butter in a small saucepan and stir in the mustard and pecans. Cook for 2 minutes, stirring constantly.

3. Pour the mustard mixture over the drained vegetables and mix well. Sprinkle with paprika and serve.

Cabbage Soup   Serves 8

1 large can (46 ounces) tomato juice
4 cups finely shredded green
  cabbage (about 1¼ pounds)
2 large carrots, peeled and shredded
1 cup thinly sliced celery,
  plus the tops chopped

1 large onion, finely chopped
Salt and black pepper
Plain yogurt
Caraway seeds

1. In a large pot, combine the tomato juice, cabbage, carrots, celery, onion, and seasonings. Bring to a boil, then reduce the heat and simmer, uncovered, for 1 hour.

2. Pour the soup into individual soup bowls and serve with a dollop of yogurt and a few caraway seeds for each person.

Sweet-and-Sour Red Cabbage   Serves 6 to 8

2 tablespoons butter
1 medium onion, thinly sliced
2 medium apples, peeled and diced

1 medium head red cabbage, shredded
1 cup Sweet and Sour Sauce (page 72)

1. Heat the butter in a large pan and sauté the onion and apples until just tender.

2. Add the cabbage, tossing lightly. Stir in the sauce and cover. Simmer until the cabbage is tender — about 15 minutes. Serve hot.

CARROTS

Carrots with Raisins   Serves 6

5 tablespoons butter
1 tablespoon granulated sugar
½ cup dry white wine
6 large carrots, peeled and thinly sliced
Grated nutmeg
Black pepper
½ cup raisins, plumped in hot water for 5 minutes, then drained

1. In a skillet with a lid, melt the butter. Add the sugar and wine and simmer very briefly.

2. Add the carrots, stirring to coat them well. Cover the skillet and cook over high heat, shaking the pan occasionally, for about 12 minutes, or until the carrots are tender-crisp and the liquid is nearly absorbed.

3. Season with nutmeg and pepper, and stir in the raisins. Serve hot.

CELERY

Cheese-Baked Celery   Serves 6 to 8

6 tablespoons butter, melted
4 cups thinly sliced celery
3 tablespoons all-purpose flour
1 cup milk
1 can (4 ounces) chopped mushrooms, drained

2 tablespoons chopped green pepper
2 tablespoons chopped pimiento
1 cup shredded sharp cheddar cheese
1 cup soft bread crumbs

1. Preheat the oven to 350 degrees.

2. Heat 4 tablespoons of butter in a large saucepan then add the celery. Sauté for about 5 minutes; it should be tender-crisp.

3. Stir in the flour, mixing well. Add the milk and cook until the mixture is smooth and thickened, stirring constantly.

4. Add the mushrooms, green pepper, pimiento, and cheese and stir until the cheese has melted.

5. Spoon the mixture into a greased 2-quart casserole.

6. Combine the bread crumbs with the remaining butter and sprinkle over the celery mixture. Bake the casserole for 20 minutes. Serve hot.

EGGPLANT

Caponata   Serves 6 to 8

½ cup olive oil
2 medium onions, chopped
2 stalks celery, chopped
1 large eggplant, chopped
8 medium tomatoes, quartered
Salt and black pepper
1½ teaspoons fresh basil or ¾ teaspoon dried
2 tablespoons tomato paste
1 cup black olives, sliced
½ cup capers, drained

1. Heat the oil in a skillet and sauté the onions and celery until golden.

2. Add the eggplant, tomatoes, seasonings, and tomato paste and toss well to combine. Continue to cook, uncovered, until the vegetables are tender. Be sure not to overcook as each vegetable should retain its own personality.

3. Stir in the olives and capers. Chill a day or so ahead of serving and serve cold as an appetizer. This will keep for a week or more in the refrigerator.

Cheese-Eggplant Purée   Serves 6

1 very large eggplant
1½ cups grated Parmesan cheese
8 tablespoons butter, melted
¼ cup finely chopped fresh parsley
Juice from 1 clove garlic
Black pepper
1 cup toasted bread crumbs

1. Preheat the oven to 375 degrees.

2. Bring salted water to a boil in a large pot. Add the eggplant whole to the water and cook for 30 minutes. Drain and peel.

3. In a mixing bowl, mash the pulp until it is smooth. Add the cheese, 6 tablespoons of butter, parsley, and seasonings. Blend thoroughly, then spoon into a lightly buttered 1½-quart baking dish.

4. Mix the remaining butter with the bread crumbs and sprinkle over the eggplant. Bake the casserole for 30 minutes, or until set.

5. Serve this with warmed pita bread or other thin, slightly firm bread. A side dish of plain yogurt makes a good addition.

Eggplant Balls   Serves 6

1 large eggplant, peeled and cut into 1-inch cubes
1 large egg
2¾ cups fresh bread crumbs, approximately
Juice from 1 clove garlic
Salt and black pepper
Oil for frying

1. Bring salted water to a boil and add the eggplant. Cook for 8 minutes, then drain in a sieve, pressing out as much liquid as possible.

2. In a large mixing bowl, mash the eggplant and then add the remaining ingredients except the oil. Shape the mixture into 36 balls.

3. Heat the oil in a skillet and sauté the balls over moderate heat, turning as necessary, until golden — about 6 to 8 minutes.

4. Drain and serve, possibly with Yogurt Mayonnaise (page 58) or Harissa Sauce (page 70).

GREEN BEANS

Braised Green Beans   Serves 4

1 pound fresh small and narrow green beans, tips removed
¼ cup olive oil
5 medium tomatoes, chopped
¼ cup chopped fresh parsley
1 tablespoon Italian Seasoning (page 48)
1 teaspoon Chili Powder (page 50)
Juice from 1 clove garlic
Grated Parmesan cheese

1. Bring salted water to a boil and cook the beans until tender-crisp — about 5 to 7 minutes. Drain the beans in a colander and rinse with cold water to stop any further cooking. Reserve.

2. In a large skillet, heat the olive oil. Add the tomatoes, parsley, and seasonings and partially cover the skillet. Simmer the mixture until the tomato liquid has evaporated and the sauce has thickened — about 20 to 25 minutes.

3. Stir in the reserved beans. Cover and simmer an additional 10 minutes.

4. Top with the grated cheese and serve hot.

Deep-Fried Green Beans

Serves 6

1 pound fresh green beans, tips removed
¼ cup all-purpose flour
Salt and black pepper
2 large eggs, lightly beaten
1 tablespoon finely grated Parmesan cheese
Vegetable oil for deep-frying

1. Bring salted water to a boil and add the beans. Cook for 5 minutes, then drain in a colander, rinse with cold water, then pat dry.

2. In a paper or plastic bag, combine the flour, salt, and pepper. Add the beans and shake to coat them.

3. In a mixing bowl, combine the eggs and cheese. Dip the floured beans into the mixture.

4. Heat the oil in a pan to 375 degrees. Deep-fry the beans, a few at a time, in the oil until they are golden — only 1 to 2 minutes should be necessary.

5. Drain the beans and serve hot.

LIMA BEANS

Lima Bean Soup   Serves 4 to 6

2 cups fresh, shelled lima beans
2 medium potatoes, chopped
1 green pepper, chopped
1 large onion, chopped
Juice from 1 clove garlic
2 tablespoons chopped fresh parsley
½ teaspoon dried thyme leaves
2 cups water or Vegetable Stock (page 76)
2 cups cottage cheese
½ cup skim milk
Sprigs of fresh parsley

1. In a large saucepan, combine the beans, potatoes, green pepper, onion, garlic juice, parsley, thyme, and stock. Bring to a boil, then reduce the heat and simmer the mixture for 30 minutes.

2. Blend the cottage cheese and milk until very smooth in a blender. Combine with the bean mixture and heat again.

3. Serve the soup in individual bowls, garnished with parsley sprigs.

MUSHROOMS

Fresh Mushroom Soup   Serves 8

1 pound fresh mushrooms
6 tablespoons butter
2 cups chopped carrots
2 cups chopped celery
1 cup chopped onion

Juice from 1 clove garlic
8 cups Vegetable Stock (page 76)
3 tablespoons tomato paste
Black pepper
3 tablespoons dry sherry

1. Chop finely half of the mushrooms. Slice the remaining and set aside.

2. In a heavy pot, heat 4 tablespoons of butter and sauté the chopped mushrooms, carrots, celery, onion, and garlic juice for 5 minutes.

3. Stir in the stock, tomato paste, and pepper and bring to a boil. Reduce the heat and simmer, covered, for 1 hour.

4. Purée the soup in a blender and then return it to the pot.

5. In a skillet, melt the remaining butter and sauté the sliced mushrooms for 5 minutes. Add the mushrooms to the soup, along with the sherry and heat. Serve hot.

Mushroom Pâté   Makes 1 quart

¼ cup butter
Juice from 1 clove garlic
1 large onion, finely chopped
1 pound fresh mushrooms, finely chopped
3 tablespoons dry sherry
2 teaspoons salt
1 teaspoon dried chervil
¾ teaspoon dried rosemary leaves
Black pepper
1⅓ cups ground walnuts
2 cups finely chopped cooked spinach
1 cup low-fat cottage cheese
2 large eggs, lightly beaten
⅓ cup minced fresh parsley
¼ teaspoon ground nutmeg

1. Preheat the oven to 375 degrees.

2. In a heavy skillet, melt the butter. Add the garlic juice, onion, and mushrooms, then sauté the mixture, stirring occasionally, for about 10 minutes.

3. Add the sherry, salt, chervil, rosemary, and pepper and continue cooking, stirring over low heat until the liquid is absorbed — about 5 to 10 minutes. Transfer the mixture to a large bowl and let it cool.

4. Add the walnuts and spinach to the cooked mushroom mixture. Toss well.

5. In a blender, mix together the cottage cheese, eggs, parsley, and nutmeg until smooth. Combine this with the mushroom mixture.

6. Butter one or more ovenproof serving dishes or a loaf pan. Spoon the mixture into the dish and smooth the top. Cover tightly with heavy-duty foil and place the dish into a larger baking pan. Add enough hot water to reach halfway up the sides of the pâté-filled container.

7. Bake the pâté for 1½ hours, then transfer the dish to a wire rack to cool.

8. Serve this pâté at room temperature. It is good spread on cheese toast.

Mushroom Chowder

Serves 6 to 8

½ cup butter
½ cup chopped onion
1 pound fresh mushrooms, sliced
1 cup diced raw potatoes
1 cup finely chopped celery
½ cup diced carrots
Black pepper
1 tablespoon all-purpose flour
2 tablespoons water
3 cups Vegetable Stock (page 76)
1 cup milk
¼ cup grated Parmesan cheese

1. Melt the butter in a skillet and sauté the onion. Add the vegetables and the pepper. Cover and simmer until the vegetables are tender — about 15 minutes.

2. Combine the flour and water in a small bowl then stir into the vegetable mixture.

3. Add the stock and simmer 10 additional minutes.

4. Stir in the milk and cheese. Cover and heat over low heat; do not let the liquid boil. Serve with an extra sprinkling of cheese if desired.

Batter-Fried Asparagus

Mushrooms Paprika   Serves 6

2 pounds fresh mushrooms, quartered
Lemon juice
6 tablespoons butter
1 medium onion, chopped
2½ tablespoons whole-wheat pastry flour
2 teaspoons paprika
Pinch of cayenne pepper
1 cup sour cream
1 cup tomato sauce
Milk

1. In a bowl, gently toss the mushrooms with just enough lemon juice to moisten the surfaces. Set aside.

2. In a large skillet, heat the butter and sauté the onion until it is translucent. Add the flour, paprika, and cayenne. Mix well.

3. Stirring constantly, mix in the sour cream and the tomato sauce; cook until the mixture is thickened and smooth. Add milk as needed for the desired consistency.

4. Add the mushrooms and cook covered, for 12 minutes.

Note: For variation, omit the tomato sauce and increase the amount of sour cream.

Baked Mushrooms   Serves 4

3½ tablespoons butter
2 tablespoons all-purpose flour
1½ cups milk or plain yogurt
½ cup dry white wine
Pinch of ground nutmeg
Black pepper
4 teaspoons minced onion

1 pound fresh mushrooms,
  thinly sliced
1 tablespoon Spicy Soy Sauce (page 72)
2 tablespoons brandy
4 slices thick toasted bread
Grated Parmesan cheese

1. Preheat the oven to 350 degrees.

2. In a saucepan, melt 1½ tablespoons butter and stir in the flour. Mix well.

3. Add the milk, wine, nutmeg, and pepper, blending thoroughly. Simmer, stirring frequently, until the sauce is thick.

4. In a skillet, sauté the onion in the remaining butter over moderate to high heat until the onion is golden. Add the mushrooms to the onion and sauté until tender — only a few minutes. Remove from the heat.

5. Add the soy sauce and brandy to the skillet. Mix well.

6. In each of 4 lightly buttered small baking dishes, put 1 slice of toast. Top with the mushroom mixture, the sauce, and the grated cheese. Bake until the cheese is bubbly — 12 to 15 minutes.

Egg and Mushroom Patties   Serves 6

7 tablespoons butter
½ teaspoon Aromatic Salt (page 47)
2 cups sliced fresh mushrooms
1 green onion or scallion, minced
3 tablespoons all-purpose flour
1 cup milk
½ teaspoon salt
2 teaspoons minced fresh parsley
6 hard-boiled eggs, finely chopped
Bread crumbs
1 large egg, lightly beaten
Vegetable oil for frying

1. In a large skillet, melt four tablespoons of butter and add the salt. Sauté the mushrooms and onion for 5 minutes. Reserve.

2. Melt three tablespoons of butter in a saucepan. Stir in the flour and blend. Add the milk, salt, and parsley to the pan and cook until the white sauce is thick. Remove from the heat.

3. Combine the mushrooms, white sauce, and chopped eggs in a mixing bowl. Add enough bread crumbs to make a moderately stiff dough. Spread the dough on a platter and, when cool, form into patties.

4. Dip the patties into the beaten egg and then into bread crumbs. Heat the oil in a skillet and then fry the patties until nicely browned on both sides.

ONIONS

A Better Onion Soup   Serves 4

2 medium onions, chopped
2 cups water
2 tablespoons butter
½ cup dry vermouth
½ teaspoon celery seeds
2 cups Vegetable Stock (page 76)
1 teaspoon onion powder
Juice from 1 clove garlic
Parmesan or mozzarella cheese

1. Simmer the onions in the water until they are tender. With a slotted spoon, remove the onions from the water (save the onion water).

2. Meanwhile, melt the butter in a skillet. When the onions are ready, add them to the skillet. Add the vermouth and celery seeds and cook over moderate heat, stirring constantly, until the liquid has evaporated and the pan feels slightly gummy. Cook very carefully until the residue on the pan begins to turn brown.

3. Add a small amount of the vegetable stock to the pan and stir to release the residue. Add this mixture to the onion water.

4. Add the remaining stock and the spices and simmer for 15 minutes.

5. Serve with grated Parmesan cheese or melted mozzarella.

Glazed Pearl Onions   Serves 4

3 tablespoons butter
20 to 24 pearl onions
¼ cup dry vermouth
2 tablespoons distilled white vinegar
3 tablespoons brown sugar
Black pepper

1. In a skillet, melt the butter. Brown the onions, shaking the pan to coat them well with the butter.

2. Add the remaining ingredients to the skillet, stirring frequently until the liquid is evaporated. The onions should be firm. Serve hot.

Nutty Onions   Serves 8

4 very large yellow onions, peeled and halved crosswise
1 cup Vegetable Stock (page 76)
2 teaspoons honey
1 teaspoon grated lemon rind
¼ teaspoon paprika
¼ cup finely chopped pecans

1. Preheat the oven to 350 degrees.

2. In a large baking dish, arrange the onion halves cut side up.

3. In a saucepan, combine the stock, honey, lemon rind, and paprika. Heat thoroughly and then pour over the onions.

4. Bake the onions, covered, for 50 minutes, or until tender.

5. When the onions are done, remove the cover and sprinkle with pecans. Continue to bake for 10 to 15 additional minutes, or until the nuts are lightly browned.

PEAS

Minted Peas   Serves 6

2½ cups shelled fresh peas
½ cup mayonnaise
¼ cup sour cream
¼ cup minced onion

¼ cup chopped fresh mint
1 teaspoon prepared mustard
Salt and black pepper
Pimiento strips

1. Bring salted water to a boil and add the peas. Cook for 1 minute, then drain and rinse with cold water.

2. Combine the mayonnaise, sour cream, onion, mint, and mustard in a mixing bowl. Add the drained peas and season with salt and pepper. Refrigerate, covered, until the dish is cold.

3. Serve the peas garnished with pimiento strips.

PEPPERS

Roasted Peppers   Serves 6

5 green peppers
5 sweet red peppers
¼ cup olive oil
¼ cup vegetable oil
¼ cup minced shallots or scallions

3 tablespoons hot prepared mustard
3 tablespoons white wine vinegar
½ teaspoon Spicy Soy Sauce (page 72)
¼ teaspoon black pepper

1. Preheat the oven to 350 degrees.

2. Bring water to a boil in a large pot. Add the peppers and cover. Cook 1 minute, then drain. Place the peppers in a large baking pan and roast in the oven for 30 minutes.

3. Cool and peel the peppers. Discard the seeds and stems and cut the peppers into strips. Place the strips in a large bowl.

4. Combine the remaining ingredients in a jar with a tight-fitting lid. Shake well to blend, then pour the dressing over the pepper strips. Toss to coat well.

5. Refrigerate the peppers, covered, overnight. Serve cold.

POTATOES

Potatoes Stuffed with Mushrooms   Serves 6

1 can (4 ounces) mushroom pieces, with liquid reserved
1½ tablespoons chopped fresh chives
1½ tablespoons bread crumbs
1 large egg, lightly beaten
Black pepper
6 large baking potatoes
2 tablespoons butter, melted

1. Preheat the oven to 400 degrees.

2. In a bowl, combine the drained mushrooms with the chives, bread crumbs, egg, and pepper. Mix well.

3. Peel the potatoes, then cut a lengthwise slice from the top of each. Set the top aside. Scoop out some of the pulp from the potatoes, making a large pocket. Fill each pocket with the prepared mushroom stuffing and replace the potato top.

4. Bake the potatoes for about 45 minutes, or until they are soft, basting them often with the reserved mushroom liquid. Serve hot.

Gnocchi (Potato Dumplings)   Serves 6

2 pounds potatoes, unpeeled
2⅓ cups all-purpose flour
Salt and white pepper
2 egg yolks

Boiling water or
    Vegetable Stock (page 76)
½ cup butter, melted
Grated Parmesan cheese

1. Cook the potatoes in water until tender. Drain, peel, and mash. Add the flour, salt, and pepper and mix.

2. Beat the egg yolks lightly, then add to the potatoes and mix to a firm, doughy consistency.

3. Place a small portion — about ½ cup — of dough onto a floured surface and shape it into a finger-thick roll. Cut the roll into pieces that are 1 inch long. Form the pieces into crescent shapes and arrange them on a lightly floured surface to dry. Continue forming the crescents until all the dough is used up.

4. In a large pan, bring water to a boil. Add the gnocchi 1 at a time until the bottom of the pan is covered. When the gnocchi rise to the surface (an occasional one may have to be nudged), remove them with a slotted spoon and drain well.

5. Place the gnocchi in a heated serving dish as they finish cooking. Pour melted butter over them, sprinkle with cheese, and serve.

Note: For variety, add chopped, cooked spinach (well drained) and a bit of lemon juice to the gnocchi dough.

SPINACH

Fried Spinach with Cheese   Serves 4 to 6

2 cups chopped fresh or frozen spinach
1 large egg
1 tablespoon wheat germ
Sprinkling of black pepper
Ground nutmeg
1 tablespoon butter
2 tablespoons grated feta cheese

1. Cook the spinach in a minimum of water just until wilted. Drain any remaining liquid.

2. In a mixing bowl, combine the spinach with the egg, wheat germ, pepper, and nutmeg.

3. Melt the butter in a small skillet and pour the spinach mixture into the pan. Fry over medium heat for 3 minutes, or until the bottom is browned.

4. Carefully turn the spinach cake over, sprinkle the top with cheese, and fry for a few minutes more.

5. Cut the spinach into wedges and serve hot.

Creamed Spinach Soup   Serves 4 to 6

3 tablespoons butter
1 medium onion, chopped
½ cup raw rice
Juice from 1 clove garlic
⅛ teaspoon ground nutmeg
6 cups Vegetable Stock (page 76)

2 pounds fresh spinach
1 cup heavy cream
Cayenne pepper
2 tablespoons lemon juice
Grated lemon rind

1. In a large pot, melt butter then add the onion. Sauté for 5 minutes.

2. Add the rice, garlic juice, and nutmeg and sauté 3 minutes, then add the stock and cook the rice until it is completely soft.

3. Add the spinach to the pot and cook just until the spinach is wilted. Purée the mixture in a blender and then return the purée to the pot.

4. Add the cream and pepper and heat gently. Just before serving, stir in the lemon juice.

5. Sprinkle each bowl with a little lemon rind and serve hot or cold.

Note: For variety, top the individual bowls of soup with a spoonful of Pesto Sauce (page 70) and a sprinkling of Parmesan cheese.

Spinach Balls   Serves 10 to 12

2 packages (10 ounces) frozen chopped spinach
3 cups herb-seasoned stuffing mix
1 large onion, finely chopped
6 large eggs, well beaten
¾ cup butter, melted
½ cup grated Parmesan cheese
1 tablespoon black pepper
Juice from 1 clove garlic
½ teaspoon dried thyme leaves

1. Preheat the oven to 325 degrees.

2. Bring salted water to a boil and cook the spinach according to the directions on the package. Drain well, squeezing to remove the excess moisture.

3. Combine the cooked spinach with the remaining ingredients in a bowl. Mix well, then shape into ¾-inch balls.

4. Place the balls on a lightly greased cookie sheet and bake for 15 to 20 minutes. Serve hot as an hors d'oeuvre.

Note: The spinach balls may be frozen before baking. Place them on a cookie sheet and freeze until firm. When frozen, remove from the cookie sheet and store in a plastic bag. When ready to use, thaw the spinach balls slightly, then bake for 20 to 25 minutes.

Spinach Loaf with Mushroom Sauce   Serves 8

LOAF:

2 pounds fresh spinach
2 tablespoons butter
¼ cup minced green onions or scallions
3 large eggs
1 cup half-and-half
½ cup bread crumbs
3 tablespoons grated Parmesan cheese
Salt and black pepper

SAUCE:

3 tablespoons butter
½ pound fresh mushrooms, sliced or quartered
1 tablespoon all-purpose flour
1 cup heavy (whipping) cream
Salt and black pepper
2 tablespoons minced fresh chives

1. Preheat the oven to 350 degrees.

2. Cook the spinach in rapidly boiling water for no more than 3 minutes. Drain thoroughly, then mince finely and place in a bowl.

3. In a skillet, melt the butter and sauté the onions for 3 minutes. Add the onions to the spinach.

4. Combine the eggs with the half-and-half and blend thoroughly. Add this to the spinach, along with the remaining ingredients.

5. Spoon the mixture into a greased 9 × 5-inch loaf pan, loosely covered with foil, and bake for 50 minutes.

6. Meanwhile, prepare the sauce. Melt the butter in a skillet and sauté the mushrooms until nicely browned. Stir in the flour.

7. Add the remaining ingredients and cook until the sauce thickens. Stir constantly to keep the sauce from burning.

8. When the loaf is ready, serve with the sauce.

Spinach Patties with Brown Sauce   Serves 4

PATTIES:

3 large eggs, lightly beaten
½ cup cooked, drained,
   and chopped spinach
½ cup finely chopped water chestnuts
¼ cup finely chopped green pepper

¼ cup finely chopped onion
Salt and black pepper
Vegetable oil for frying

SAUCE:

2 tablespoons butter
4 teaspoons cornstarch
2 teaspoons granulated sugar

1 cup water
3 tablespoons Spicy Soy
   Sauce (page 72)

1. In a large mixing bowl, combine all the ingredients for the patties except the vegetable oil. Shape the mixture into 4 patties.

2. Heat the oil over medium to high heat and brown the patties on both sides.

3. While the patties brown, melt the butter in a saucepan and stir in the cornstarch.

4. Add the remaining sauce ingredients to the saucepan. Cook and stir until thickened.

5. Serve the patties hot, with the brown sauce.

Spinach Dumplings   Serves 6

3 packages (10 ounces) frozen chopped spinach, thawed and pressed dry
1 pound ricotta or low-fat cottage cheese
4 egg yolks
1½ cups grated Parmesan cheese
½ teaspoon ground nutmeg
Black pepper
Flour for dusting
Water or Vegetable Stock (page 76)
¼ cup butter, melted

1. In a large mixing bowl, combine the spinach, ricotta, egg yolks, 1 cup of Parmesan cheese, nutmeg, and pepper. Blend well, then shape into 1-inch balls. Lightly coat the balls with flour, but do not allow the balls to touch one another.

2. Bring water or stock to a boil and place a few balls at a time into the pot. As each ball rises to the surface — it should take less than 1 minute to do so — remove it with a slotted spoon. Place the cooked dumplings in a well-buttered baking dish.

3. Preheat the oven to 350 degrees as you cook the dumplings.

4. When all the dumplings are cooked, pour the melted butter over them and sprinkle with the remaining grated cheese. Bake the dumplings, covered, until hot.

Spinach Ring   Serves 6

2 tablespoons butter
1 medium onion, chopped
1 large stalk celery, chopped
½ green pepper, chopped
2 packages (10 ounces) frozen chopped spinach, thawed and pressed dry
Grated rind and juice of 1 small lemon
Pinch of ground nutmeg
¼ teaspoon black pepper
1⅓ cups bread crumbs
⅔ cup milk
3 large eggs, beaten

1. Preheat the oven to 375 degrees.

2. In a large skillet, melt the butter. Sauté the onion, celery, and pepper until wilted.

3. Add the remaining ingredients and mix well.

4. Spoon the mixture into a buttered 1-quart ring mold. Place the mold in a pan of hot water and bake until set — about 40 minutes.

5. Unmold the ring onto a warmed serving platter and fill the center with cooked rice.

Borani

Serves 4 to 6

2 pounds fresh spinach, coarsely chopped
1 large onion, grated
2 cups plain yogurt, beaten
2 tablespoons olive oil
1 tablespoon lemon juice
¼ teaspoon black pepper
Juice from 1 clove garlic
½ cup chopped walnuts
1 tablespoon toasted sesame seeds
2 tablespoons minced fresh mint
Lemon wedges

1. In a large pot, combine the spinach and onion. Cover and steam for 5 minutes, then strain in a colander. Place the mixture in a wooden bowl.

2. Add the yogurt, olive oil, lemon juice, pepper, garlic juice, and walnuts. Toss and chill.

3. Just before serving, sprinkle with sesame seeds and mint. Garnish with lemon wedges, and serve with extra yogurt if desired.

Hot Spinach Salad   Serves 6

2 pounds fresh spinach, torn into bite-sized pieces
6 hard-boiled eggs, sliced
Black pepper
2 tablespoons imitation bacon bits
¾ cup vegetable oil
½ cup cider vinegar
¼ cup lemon juice
4 teaspoons granulated sugar
1 teaspoon Worcestershire sauce
¼ pound fresh mushrooms, thinly sliced
1½ ounces 100-proof brandy

1. Place the spinach in a large salad bowl and arrange the egg slices on top. Sprinkle with pepper.

2. Mix together in a saucepan the remaining ingredients except the brandy. Heat until very hot.

3. Meanwhile, heat the brandy in another container and add it to the mushroom mixture and ignite. Pour the flaming dressing over the spinach and eggs, and toss gently but thoroughly. Serve on warmed salad plates.

TOMATOES

Stuffed Tomatoes   Serves 8

1 pound yellow squash
1 pound zucchini
2 teaspoons salt
8 large tomatoes
Vegetable oil
Black pepper

4 tablespoons butter
1 medium onion, minced
1 cup heavy cream
Juice from 1 clove garlic
½ cup grated gruyère cheese
¼ cup grated Parmesan cheese

1. Preheat the oven to 325 degrees.

2. Grate the squash and spread it in a large colander. Sprinkle with the salt, toss, and let stand for 30 minutes. Squeeze out the moisture.

3. Cut a ¾-inch slice from the top of the tomatoes. With a small spoon, remove the seeds and any juice without breaking the walls of the tomatoes. Brush the outside of the tomatoes with oil and sprinkle with pepper.

4. Bake the tomatoes, cut-side up, for 10 minutes. Remove the tomatoes from the oven, invert them on a rack, and let them drain for at least 30 minutes.

5. In a skillet, melt the butter and sauté the onion over moderately high heat. Add the drained squash and continue to cook, stirring, for 2 minutes. Stir in the cream and garlic juice and cook until the cream has been absorbed. Remove the pan from the heat and stir in both cheeses.

6. Divide the mixture among the tomatoes, mounding it, and sprinkling with additional Parmesan cheese if desired.

7. Broil the filled tomatoes on the rack of a broiler about 5 inches from the heat for 3 to 4 minutes, or until the tops are bubbly and golden. Serve hot.

ZUCCHINI

Zucchini Parmesan   Serves 4

4 medium zucchini
3 tablespoons Garlic Butter (page 53)
Pinch of dried oregano
Black pepper
⅔ cup grated Parmesan cheese

1. Steam the whole zucchinis until they are tender-crisp — about 8 to 10 minutes. Slice them lengthwise into ¼-inch-thick slices.

2. In a bowl, combine the butter and spices. Spread this on the zucchini slices and place the slices on a baking sheet. Sprinkle the slices with cheese.

3. Broil the zucchini about 5 inches from the heat source and until they are golden. Serve hot.

Zucchini Patties

Serves 4

2 cups coarsely grated zucchini
2 large eggs, lightly beaten
¼ cup minced onion
¼ to ½ cup all-purpose flour, as needed
¼ cup grated Parmesan cheese
½ teaspoon baking powder
Salt and black pepper
¼ teaspoon dried oregano
Vegetable oil
Lemon Butter (page 54), melted

1. Place the zucchini in a strainer and press out as much moisture as possible.

2. Mix the zucchini with the eggs and onion in a large mixing bowl.

3. Combine the flour, cheese, baking powder, and seasonings and add to the zucchini mixture. Shape into 4 patties.

4. Heat the oil over medium heat and fry the patties until lightly browned on both sides. Drain the cooked patties and drizzle with butter. Serve immediately.

Zucchini Flan   Serves 6 to 8

7 small zucchini, cut into narrow strips
1 teaspoon salt
2 tablespoons vegetable oil
4 large eggs, lightly beaten
⅓ cup grated Parmesan cheese
½ cup grated feta cheese
½ cup finely chopped fresh parsley
¼ teaspoon dried oregano
Black pepper

1. Place the zucchini strips in a colander. Sprinkle with salt, toss gently, and then set aside for 30 minutes. Drain and pat dry.

2. Preheat the oven to 375 degrees.

3. Heat the oil in a heavy skillet. Add the zucchini, cover, and steam until just heated through — about 2 to 3 minutes.

4. Place the zucchini in an 8-inch baking dish, laying the strips across the bottom to fit snugly.

5. Combine the remaining ingredients in a bowl and then pour over the zucchini. Bake until lightly browned — about 30 minutes. Serve hot.

Zucchini French Fries   Serves 1 to 2

Vegetable oil for frying
1 medium zucchini, cut into strips
Whole-wheat flour for dredging
Aromatic Salt (page 47)

1. Heat the oil to 375 degrees.

2. Dredge the zucchini strips with the flour, shaking off excess. Fry in the hot oil until lightly browned.

3. Drain the zucchini on paper towels and sprinkle with salt.

MIXED VEGETABLES

Meatless Loaf   Serves 6

¼ cup vegetable oil
1 cup chopped onion
1 cup any combination of diced celery, green pepper, fresh parsley,
    drained and seeded tomatoes, carrots, squash, cooked dried beans,
    olives, etc.
1 cup finely chopped nuts of your choice or 1 cup chunk-style peanut
    butter
1 cup cooked rice
⅓ cup bread crumbs
1 cup grated cheese
2 large eggs, lightly beaten
Black pepper

1. Preheat the oven to 350 degrees.

2. Heat the oil in a skillet and sauté the vegetables until limp.

3. Combine the sautéed vegetables with the remaining ingredients. Mix
    well, adding a small amount of liquid if the mixture seems too dry.

4. Pour the mixture into a greased loaf pan and bake for 40 minutes.
    Serve hot or cold.

Vegetables in a Shell   Serves 6

2 large eggs
½ cup all-purpose flour
½ cup half-and-half
¼ teaspoon salt
3 tablespoons butter
1 pound fresh mushrooms, quartered
½ pound carrots, peeled and cut into ¼-inch slices
½ cup sliced black olives
½ teaspoon chopped fresh dill
1 teaspoon dried savory
¼ pound grated gouda cheese
Additional grated cheese (optional)
Alfalfa sprouts

1. Preheat the oven to 450 degrees.

2. Heat a 9-inch skillet on the lowest shelf of the oven until it is very hot. Meanwhile, mix together the eggs, flour, half-and-half, and salt. Beat until the mixture is smooth.

3. Remove the skillet from the oven and add 1 tablespoon butter. Rotate the pan until the butter melts and coats the bottom and sides completely. Add the batter immediately, again rotating the pan slightly.

4. Bake the pancake on the lowest shelf of the oven for 10 minutes, then reduce the heat to 350 degrees and continue to bake until the shell is golden — about 10 minutes. Remove from the oven.

5. While the shell is baking, melt the remaining butter and sauté the vegetables for 5 minutes. Add the olives, spices, and cheese and continue to cook, stirring constantly, until the cheese melts.

6. Spoon the vegetable mixture into the shell, sprinkle with the additional cheese, and place the pan under the broiler for about 2 minutes.

7. Remove from the broiler, top with sprouts, and serve immediately.

CHAPTER

7

Dried Beans for All Occasions

DRIED BEANS FOR ALL OCCASIONS

Dried beans form the basis for much of the vegetarian diet. In all vegetarian cookbooks you will find countless recipes using beans as an ingredient for soups, loafs, rice dishes, or vegetable medleys. It is likely you already use some dried beans in your cooking, but you can develop even more possibilities when you know about the many more dried beans that are available. A trip to your supermarket or natural foods store will open up for you the wondrous and varied characteristics of black beans, dried black- and yellow-eyed peas, canellini (white kidney beans), garbanzos (chick peas), cranberry beans (roman beans), fava beans, pinto beans, white beans, and soybeans. The last — soybeans — are the source of an almost endless variety of products used in Oriental cooking. If you have ever eaten tofu, or even soy sauce, then you have had a soybean product (see pages 192–194).

COOKING WITH DRIED BEANS

In order to use dried beans, you must soak them ahead of time in water or else allow additional cooking time so that they can replenish the moisture lost in the drying process. In most cases, you will probably choose to set the beans out the night before, but there is also a quick-soaking method if you forget.

Mujaddarah

1. Overnight soaking. Rinse the beans and remove any that are too shriveled to be revitalized. Also check for extraneous matter, such as tiny stones. For each pound of dried beans, add 6 cups of water. Soak overnight, then drain and rinse. Soybeans should be refrigerated during the soaking period to prevent fermentation.

2. Quick soaking. Rinse the beans and go through the same process of sorting as given in the previous paragraph. For each pound of dried beans, bring 8 cups of water to a boil. Add the beans and boil for 2 minutes. Remove the beans from the stove, cover the pan, and allow to soak for 1 hour. Drain and rinse the beans.

Most dried beans, after they are soaked, will cook in 1½ to 2½ hours, although garbanzos require more time and lentils less. To cook, cover the beans with water and add 1 teaspoon of salt or other seasoning per cup of beans. The addition of 1 tablespoon of vegetable oil per cup of beans will reduce the foam that results when the beans cook. Beans should be partially covered and cooked over low heat. Stir gently, preferably with a wooden spoon, to keep the beans from breaking. The beans will approximately double in volume, from the dried state to the cooked.

Beans may be cooked when you have the time and then stored in the refrigerator for up to a week, or kept in the freezer for many months if wrapped tightly.

The following recipes are suggestions as to how best use the various types of beans. Many times you can substitute one type of bean for another quite successfully.

Black Bean Bisque with Sherry   Serves 4

3 cups water
¾ cup dried black beans
¼ teaspoon dried oregano
⅛ teaspoon ground cumin
1 bay leaf
1 clove garlic
2 tablespoons vegetable oil

1 stalk celery, diced
1 medium onion, diced
1 medium carrot, peeled and diced
1 medium tomato, diced
Black pepper
2 cups Vegetable Stock (page 76)
4 tablespoons dry sherry

1. Combine the first 6 ingredients in a large pot. Bring to a boil, then lower the heat and simmer, covered, until the beans are tender — about 2 to 2½ hours for beans that have not been presoaked, less time if they have been presoaked. Remove and discard the bay leaf and garlic. Set the beans aside.

2. In a skillet, heat the oil and sauté the vegetables. Sprinkle with pepper and cook until just tender — about 5 minutes. Add the skillet mixture to the beans in the pot.

3. Purée the beans and vegetables in small batches in a blender. Combine the purée with the stock in a saucepan and simmer until the mixture is heated through. Stir occasionally to keep the mixture from burning.

4. When ready to serve, pour the soup into individual bowls. Stir 1 tablespoon of sherry into each bowl.

Variation: After puréeing the bean-vegetable mixture and combining it with the stock, add ½ pound raw shrimp (if you eat shellfish), shelled and cut into ½-inch pieces. Simmer the soup just long enough to cook the shrimp, then serve with the sherry, as noted above.

Garbanzo Pâté   Serves 8 to 12

2 cups cooked garbanzo beans
¼ cup reserved cooking liquid from the beans, or ¼ cup stock
1 cup minced fresh parsley
½ cup tahini
5 tablespoons lemon juice
¼ cup olive oil
Juice from 1 clove garlic
½ teaspoon ground cumin
½ teaspoon cayenne pepper
Salt
Sliced black olives (optional)

1. Purée the cooked beans, using the liquid as needed to make a smooth purée.

2. Combine the purée with the remaining ingredients except the olives. The mixture should be thick.

3. Chill, covered, for at least 1 hour. Garnish with olives, if desired, and serve as an hors d'oeuvre with whole-wheat bread toast and pickles.

Black Bean Soup with Rice — Serves 6 to 8

1 pound dried black beans
2 quarts water
1½ tablespoons salt
Juice from 1 clove garlic
4 tablespoons distilled white vinegar
1½ teaspoons ground cumin
1½ teaspoons dried oregano
½ cup + 1 tablespoon olive oil
1 large onion, chopped, + 2 tablespoons finely chopped onion
1 large green pepper, chopped
1 cup cooked rice

1. In a large kettle, soak the beans overnight in the water. After soaking, add the salt and bring to a boil. Cover, reduce the heat, and simmer until the beans are cooked — about 1½ hours. Stir occasionally. Set aside.

2. In a small bowl, combine the garlic juice, 2 tablespoons vinegar, cumin, and oregano. Set aside.

3. Heat ½ cup of oil in a skillet and sauté the 1 chopped onion and the green pepper for 5 minutes. Add the reserved garlic mixture and continue to cook for 2 minutes more.

4. Add the skillet mixture to the kettle with the beans and simmer, covered, for 1 hour. Stir occasionally.

5. Combine the remaining onion, vinegar, olive oil, and rice in a small bowl. Cover and marinate at least 2 hours at room temperature.

6. To serve, ladle the soup into individual bowls and add a generous tablespoon of the marinated rice mixture to each. Serve immediately.

Greek Lentil Soup   Serves 6 to 8

2 quarts Vegetable Stock (page 76)
1 cup dried lentils
1 medium onion, chopped
1 stalk celery, chopped

1 bay leaf
¼ teaspoon dried oregano
3 tablespoons tomato paste
2 tablespoons wine vinegar

1. Bring the stock to a boil in a large saucepan.

2. Without disturbing the boil, slowly pour the lentils into the vigorously boiling stock.

3. Add all the remaining ingredients except the vinegar. Reduce the heat and simmer, stirring occasionally, until the lentils are very soft — about 1½ hours.

4. Remove the soup from the heat and add the vinegar. Discard the bay leaf.

5. Purée half of the soup. Return the puréed portion to the pan. Mix, heat again, and serve.

Black Beans with Rice   Serves 4 to 6

1 cup dried black beans
2 medium tomatoes, cored and halved
1 large onion, halved, + 1 large onion, thinly sliced
1 tablespoon Middle Eastern Spice (page 47)
Juice from 1 clove garlic
½ cup vegetable oil
1 teaspoon Italian Seasoning (page 48)
1½ cups raw rice
½ cup dry sherry
1 green pepper, thinly sliced
1 sweet red pepper, thinly sliced

1. Soak the beans in water to cover overnight.

2. Transfer the soaked beans, along with the water, to a kettle. Add enough additional water to cover the beans by 2 inches. Add the tomatoes, onion halves, Middle Eastern Spice, and garlic juice and simmer, covered, for 1 hour. Drain the beans and reserve both beans and liquid.

3. Preheat the oven to 350 degrees.

4. In another pan, heat ¼ cup of oil, add the seasoning and the rice, and stir to coat the rice. Add the sherry and enough of the reserved cooking liquid to barely cover the rice. Simmer, covered, for 10 minutes.

5. Transfer the rice to a 3-quart baking dish and add the beans, stirring to mix with the rice. Bake, covered, in a 350-degree oven for 20 minutes. When finished, allow to stand for 10 minutes.

6. While the rice is baking, sauté the peppers and remaining onion in the remaining oil until the vegetables are wilted. Spread this mixture over the baked rice and beans and serve.

Bean with Barley Soup   Serves 4 to 6

2 tablespoons butter
½ cup chopped onion
1 cup peeled and diced carrots
2 cups peeled and diced potatoes
6 cups Vegetable Stock (page 76)

Juice from 1 clove garlic
½ teaspoon black pepper
1 cup cooked white beans
   (navy or great northern)
¼ cup barley

1. Melt the butter in a large pot. Sauté the onion until wilted.

2. Add the next 5 ingredients. Bring to a boil and then reduce the heat. Simmer until the vegetables are tender, then remove from the heat and purée in a blender.

3. Return the purée to the pot. Add the beans and barley. Simmer until the barley is tender — 45 minutes to 1 hour. Stir occasionally, adding more stock if necessary.

Black Bean Lasagne

Serves 8

2 cups Spaghetti Sauce (page 68)
1½ cups cooked black beans
4 lasagne noodles, cooked (or enough to fit a baking dish)
2 cups ricotta or low-fat cottage cheese
¾ pound mozzarella cheese, grated
½ cup grated Parmesan cheese

1. Preheat the oven to 375 degrees.

2. Spoon a small amount of the sauce into the bottom of a baking dish.

3. Combine the rest of the sauce with the cooked beans.

4. Assemble the lasagne in a 7½ × 12-inch baking dish. Lay down 2 noodles, then follow with the beans and sauce, then the ricotta, the mozzarella, and the Parmesan cheeses. Repeat, using the remaining 2 noodles; end with the Parmesan cheese.

5. Bake for 20 minutes, then serve.

Tamale Bean Pie   Serves 6

2 cups cooked kidney beans
1 tablespoon tomato paste
3 tablespoons water
2 tablespoons vegetable oil
½ cup chopped onion
3 teaspoons Chili Powder (page 50)
½ cup corn, fresh or canned (drained)

Juice from 1 clove garlic
¼ cup sliced black olives
1 green pepper, chopped
1½ cups cornmeal
2½ cups cold water
½ cup grated cheddar cheese

1. Place the kidney beans, tomato paste, and water in a blender and purée.

2. In a large, heavy skillet, heat the oil and sauté the onion until wilted. Add the bean purée, the garlic juice, 2 teaspoons of chili powder, olives, corn, and green pepper. Stir until well mixed and heated through.

3. Preheat the oven to 350 degrees.

4. Combine the cornmeal, cold water, and remaining chili powder in a heavy pan. Cook over medium heat, stirring constantly to prevent sticking, until the mixture thickens and comes to a boil.

5. Pour two-thirds of the cornmeal mixture into a greased 8 × 8-inch pan. Top with the bean mixture, and then the remaining cornmeal. Sprinkle the cheese over the top and bake for 30 minutes. Serve hot.

Felafel with Tahini Sauce   Serves 6

FELAFEL:

¼ cup bulgur
Hot water
2 cups cooked garbanzo
   beans, mashed
Juice from 1 clove garlic
1 teaspoon salt
¼ teaspoon turmeric
1½ teaspoons Conserie D'Harissa (page 50)

1 tablespoon minced fresh parsley
3 tablespoons bread crumbs
1 large egg, beaten
Flour for coating
Vegetable oil for deep-frying

SAUCE:

1 cup tahini
1 cup lemon juice
2 tablespoons vegetable oil
1 tablespoon Salad Herbs (page 49)

½ teaspoon salt
Juice from 1 clove garlic
Black pepper

1. Prepare the felafel. Soak the bulgur in hot water to cover for 20 minutes. Drain off any unabsorbed water.

2. Combine the bulgur with the next 8 ingredients. Chill, then shape into 12 balls. Roll the balls in flour and deep-fry in hot oil until golden. Drain.

3. Combine all the ingredients for the sauce to a smooth pastelike consistency.

4. Serve the felafel with the sauce poured lightly over each.

Kidney Beans in Red Wine   Serves 6

2 cups dried kidney beans
1 tablespoon Italian
   Seasoning (page 48)
2 tablespoons butter

1 small onion, chopped
2 tablespoons all-purpose flour
Black pepper
1 cup dry red wine

1. Soak the beans overnight in water or stock to cover.

2. Place the beans and the soaking liquid in a large saucepan. Add the seasoning and simmer for about 2 hours. Drain the beans and keep them hot.

3. Melt the butter in a skillet and sauté the onion. Add the flour and pepper, stirring until smooth. Add the wine and cook until the sauce thickens, stirring constantly.

4. Add the beans to the skillet and mix well.

Variation: Add some sliced mushrooms to the skillet as you sauté the onion, for a wine-mushroom sauce.

Baked Chili Beans   Serves 8

1 pound dried kidney beans
4½ cups water
2 tablespoons vegetable oil
1 green pepper, chopped
2 medium onions, chopped

Juice from 1 clove garlic
1 tablespoon Chili Powder (page 50)
1 can (15 ounces) tomato sauce
1 cup shredded sharp cheddar cheese

1. Combine the beans and water in a bowl and let stand uncovered for 8 hours or overnight.

2. In a large, heavy saucepan, heat the oil and sauté the green pepper and onions for 3 minutes.

3. Add the beans, soaking liquid, garlic juice, and chili powder to the pot. Bring to a boil and then reduce the heat. Simmer, covered, until the beans are almost tender — about 1 to 1½ hours.

4. Preheat the oven to 350 degrees.

5. Stir the tomato sauce into the cooked bean mixture and transfer to a baking dish. Bake, covered, until the beans are completely tender — about 1 hour, 15 minutes.

6. Remove the cover, sprinkle with cheese, and continue to bake, uncovered, another 15 minutes. Serve.

Curried Lentils   Serves 6

1 cup dried lentils
2 cups Vegetable Stock (page 76)
2 tablespoons butter
1 medium onion, sliced
¼ cup diced celery
1 tablespoon Curry Powder (page 48)
1 tablespoon all-purpose flour
¼ cup dry white wine
Black pepper

1. Cook the lentils in the stock, covered, for about 30 minutes. Drain and reserve lentils and any remaining liquid.

2. Melt the butter in a skillet. Add the onion, celery, curry powder, and any remaining stock. Cover and simmer 10 minutes.

3. Stir in the flour and wine, blending well. Add the lentils and pepper. Simmer, covered, just until hot, then serve.

Mujaddarah   Serves 8

3¾ cups Vegetable Stock (page 76)
Juice from 1 clove garlic
¼ teaspoon black pepper
1 cup dried lentils
1 cup bulgur
¼ cup olive oil
2 medium onions, sliced lengthwise
8 medium tomatoes, cut into bite-sized pieces
½ cup chopped fresh parsley
6 scallions, thinly sliced
Juice from 1 large lemon

1. Combine the stock and spices in a large pot and bring to a boil. Add the lentils and bulgur, then reduce the heat to low and simmer, covered, until the liquid is absorbed — about 15 minutes.

2. While the lentils and bulgur are cooking, heat the oil in a skillet and sauté the onions until wilted.

3. When the lentil mixture is ready, combine with the onions.

4. In a bowl, blend the remaining ingredients. And now for the surprise. The hot lentil-bulgur-onion mixture is served over the tomato mixture!

North African Rice with Spinach and Lentils

Serves 8

12 tablespoons butter
1½ cups minced onions + 2 onions, thinly sliced in rings
4 cups cooked lentils
4 cups cooked rice
3 pounds fresh spinach, shredded

1. Heat 4 tablespoons of butter in a large skillet. Sauté 1 cup of minced onion until wilted, then add the lentils and rice until heated through.

2. In another skillet, heat 4 tablespoons of butter and sauté ½ cup of onion briefly, then add the spinach and cook until wilted. Combine the spinach with the rice-lentil mixture.

3. In another skillet, heat 4 more tablespoons of butter and sauté the onion rings until wilted.

4. To serve, mound the onion-spinach-rice mixture on a large serving platter. Top with the sautéed onion rings.

Lentil and Bulgur Pilaf   Serves 6

12 tablespoons butter
1 cup minced onion
2 cups cooked lentils
1 cup softened bulgur
¼ cup minced fresh parsley
1 teaspoon Middle Eastern Spice (page 47)
½ cup pine nuts

1. Melt 6 tablespoons of butter in a skillet and brown the onion. Add the lentils, bulgur, parsley, and spice. Heat thoroughly, stirring constantly.

2. In a separate skillet, melt the remaining butter. Add the pine nuts and sauté until the nuts are browned.

3. To serve, mound the lentil-bulgur mixture on a heated serving platter. Top with the toasted pine nuts.

Lentil and Spinach Pilaf   Serves 4

6 tablespoons butter
1 pound fresh spinach, finely chopped
Juice from 1 clove garlic
1½ cups cooked lentils
1 tablespoon chopped fresh parsley
¼ teaspoon black pepper
¼ teaspoon ground cumin

1. Melt 3 tablespoons of butter in a skillet, then add the spinach. Sauté the spinach until wilted.

2. Add the rest of the ingredients except the remaining butter. Sauté just until ingredients are blended well and heated through — about 4 to 5 minutes; do not overcook.

3. Place the mixture on a heated platter. Melt the remaining butter and drizzle on the pilaf. Serve immediately.

Lentil and Spinach Squares   Serves 6

2 cups cooked lentils
2 cups cooked spinach, drained and chopped
1 cup plain yogurt
1 cup evaporated milk
2 medium onions, chopped
½ cup bread crumbs
1 teaspoon dried sage
2 egg whites, stiffly beaten

1. Preheat the oven to 350 degrees.

2. Partially mash the lentils and combine them with the other
ingredients except the egg whites.

3. Fold in the egg whites. Spread the mixture flat in an oiled
7½ × 12-inch rectangular baking dish and bake for 45 minutes.
Cut in squares and serve hot.

Lentil Burgers   Serves 4 to 6

2 cups cooked lentils
1 cup soft whole-wheat bread crumbs
½ cup wheat germ
½ cup finely chopped onion
Salt
2 whole eggs, lightly beaten
Dash of Tabasco sauce
3 tablespoons vegetable oil

1. In a medium bowl, mash the lentils slightly.

2. Add the remaining ingredients except the oil; shape into patties.

3. Heat the oil in a heavy skillet. Fry the patties until golden brown on both sides — about 5 minutes.

4. Serve with tomatoes and shredded lettuce in whole-wheat pita bread or on whole-wheat hamburger buns.

Lentil-Nut Loaf   Serves 6

3 tablespoons vegetable oil
1 medium onion, finely chopped
½ cup wheat germ
2 cups cooked lentils
½ cup bread crumbs
½ cup chopped walnuts
½ teaspoon dried sage
2 whole eggs, beaten
½ cup Vegetable Stock (page 76)

1. Preheat the oven to 350 degrees.

2. Heat the oil in a large skillet. Sauté the onion until wilted.

3. In a bowl, combine the onion with the other ingredients. Place in a greased loaf pan. Cover with foil and bake for 30 minutes.

4. Uncover and continue to bake for an additional 10 minutes. Serve.

Kusherie   Serves 6 to 8

4 cups Vegetable Stock (page 76)
4 tablespoons vegetable oil
1¼ cups dried lentils
Black pepper
1½ cups raw rice
3½ cups tomato sauce
3 medium onions, sliced
Juice from 1 clove garlic

1. Bring the stock to a boil.

2. Heat 2 tablespoons of oil in a heavy saucepan or covered skillet. Add the lentils and cook for about 5 minutes, over medium heat, stirring often. Add the boiling stock, the pepper, and the rice. Reduce the heat to low, cover the pan, and simmer 25 minutes without stirring.

3. While the lentils and rice are cooking, heat the tomato sauce gently, stirring to keep it from sticking.

4. Also meanwhile, heat the remaining oil in a small skillet. Add the onions and garlic juice and sauté until the onions are light brown.

5. Put the rice-lentil mixture on a heated platter. Cover with tomato sauce and top with browned onions. Serve.

Variation: Omit the tomato sauce, but not the browned onions, and serve with plain yogurt.

Bourbon-Baked Beans   Serves 8

½ cup chopped onion
2 cans (16 ounces) baked beans with liquid
⅓ cup molasses
¼ cup bourbon
¼ cup strong coffee
1 teaspoon Conserie D'Harissa (page 50) or Chili Powder (page 50)
¼ cup brown sugar
1 can (8 ounces) pineapple chunks, drained

1. Preheat the oven to 375 degrees.

2. Combine all ingredients in a large bowl except the sugar and pineapple. Blend well. Spoon into a 1½-quart casserole. Cover and bake for 45 minutes.

3. Sprinkle the beans with the sugar and pineapple chunks. Continue to bake, uncovered, an additional 40 minutes. Serve.

8

Bean Sprouts and Soybean Products

BEAN SPROUTS AND SOYBEAN PRODUCTS

In this chapter, I focus on some relatively new additions to the American diet. Sprouts, made from soybeans or any of a number of other grains, are now commonplace in most supermarkets. Miso, tempeh, and tofu are still a bit rare, although tofu is rapidly becoming more visible. If you haven't tried them yet, why not do it now?

BEAN SPROUTS

If you have never tried sprouting your own, you might want to start. It is simple, fun, and economical. There is no end to the uses of sprouts — either as a substitute for lettuce or in an endless number of Chinese-style dishes.

Almost all whole seeds or beans will sprout, but make sure that you never eat potato sprouts — they are poisonous. Sprouts will reach their optimum length in two to five days, depending on the seed or bean used. The following recipe uses alfalfa seeds, which will sprout and reach their maximum length (¾ to 1 inch) in three to four days. Alfalfa sprouts are especially delicately flavored, and they are great on sandwiches in place of lettuce or in a variety of salads.

You can grow sprouts in any container that is suitable for storing food, but sprouting is easiest in a wide-mouth glass jar. That way you can watch them grow, besides! I use a quart-size mason jar, the top for which I have altered slightly. I removed the center seal, used it as a pattern, and replaced it with a piece of rust-proof window screening.

Alfalfa Sprouts   Makes 2 cups

1 tablespoon alfalfa seeds
Water

1. Place the seeds in the container. Cover with water and let soak overnight.

2. The next day, place a piece of screening on top of the jar and secure with the lid or lay a piece of cheesecloth or other porous cloth over the top. If using cloth, secure it with a rubber band. Drain off the water, then run water into the container to rinse the seeds. Drain off the water.

3. Set the container with the seeds aside to sprout. Do not place them in direct sunlight, but almost anywhere else is fine. The sprouts will be greener and prettier if they are allowed to grow in the light rather than in a cabinet. (I keep mine near the kitchen sink so that I won't forget about them.)

4. Continue rinsing and draining the seeds at least twice a day until they have reached ¾ to 1 inch in length (3 to 4 days). At this point, place them in direct sunlight for just a few hours to develop the chlorophyll and to heighten their green color.

5. Put the sprouts in cold water briefly and separate them so that they will be easier to use later. The sprouts may be stored for about 1 week in a covered container, kept in the refrigerator.

Note: By the third day you will probably notice that some seeds just aren't going to sprout. These "dead" seeds can be thrown away if you wish, but this is really not necessary. When your alfalfa sprouts are ready, and you have placed them in the cold water, the sprouts will shed their skins. Once again it is up to you as to whether you wish to throw these skins away. Neither the seeds nor the hulls will mar the flavor or texture of the sprouts.

Mung Bean Sprouts   Makes 2 to 3 cups

¼ cup mung beans
Water

1. Soak the beans overnight in the sprouting container, then rinse and follow instructions for preparing alfalfa sprouts.

2. The mung beans will sprout and reach their optimum length of 1½ to 2 inches in 3 to 5 days.

Note: In contrast to the note on the alfalfa seeds, you will want to discard the mung beans that do not sprout and will also want to discard the hulls when they are shed.

Sweet-and-Sour Sprouts   Serves 4

1 cup Vegetable Stock (page 76)
1 teaspoon Spicy Soy Sauce (page 72)
1 can (9 ounces) pineapple chunks, with juice
1 tablespoon cider vinegar
1 teaspoon prepared mustard
2 tablespoons cornstarch
2 tablespoons cold water
1 green pepper, thinly sliced
1 large tomato, cubed
2 cups mung bean sprouts
4 cups hot cooked rice

1. In a skillet, combine the stock, soy sauce, juice from the pineapple, vinegar, and mustard. Mix well and heat thoroughly.

2. Combine the cornstarch with the water and then stir that into the skillet mixture. Simmer, stirring constantly, until the sauce starts to thicken.

3. Add the remaining ingredients, except the rice. Simmer until thoroughly heated. Serve over the hot rice.

Sprouts with Spiced Eggs   Serves 8

¼ cup + 4 tablespoons vegetable oil
2 tablespoons Chili Powder (page 50)
Juice from 1 clove garlic
½ teaspoon ground ginger
1 large tomato, peeled and diced
2 teaspoons distilled white vinegar

½ cup water
3 tablespoons Spice Soy
  Sauce (page 72)
8 hard-boiled eggs, shelled
4 cups mung bean sprouts
1 cup minced shallots or scallions

1. Heat ¼ cup of oil in a saucepan and add the chili powder, garlic juice, and ginger. Cook over low heat for 8 minutes.

2. Add the tomato and continue to cook for 3 minutes.

3. Add ¼ cup water, the vinegar, and the soy sauce and remove the pan from the heat.

4. Lightly scratch the surface of the eggs with a fork, being careful not to make deep cuts into the interior. Heat 2 tablespoons of the oil in a skillet and add the eggs. Sauté over low heat, turning frequently until the eggs are golden — about 2 minutes. Drain the eggs on paper toweling.

5. Add the sautéed eggs to the saucepan, stirring to coat them. Return the pan to the stove and cook over low heat for 5 minutes, adding up to ¼ cup additional water if needed to thin the sauce.

6. In another skillet, heat the remaining oil and sauté the sprouts and shallot for 5 minutes.

7. Serve the spiced eggs atop the sprout mixture.

Hot Bean Sprout Salad   Serves 4

1 tablespoon vegetable oil
4 scallions, thinly sliced, greens included
8 large fresh mushrooms, thinly sliced
4 cups mung bean sprouts
1 can (4 ounces) bamboo shoots, cut into matchsticks
¼ cup Spicy Soy Sauce (page 72)
2 tablespoons peanut butter (optional)
1 teaspoon granulated sugar or honey
2 tablespoons dry sherry
1 tablespoon prepared mustard

1. Heat the vegetable oil in a large skillet. Add the scallions and mushrooms and stir-fry until limp.

2. Add the bean sprouts and bamboo shoots to the skillet. Stir to mix well.

3. Combine the remaining ingredients in a small bowl. Pour the mixture into the skillet and continue to stir-fry until all ingredients are coated. When thoroughly heated, serve.

MISO

Miso (pronounced *MEE-zo*), or fermented soybean paste, should be used sparingly, mainly as a seasoning. Its relatively high salt content calls for caution in the amount used. Miso comes in a variety of colors, with each type having its own distinctive flavor and aroma. The darker varieties are hearty, while the lighter ones are subtly sweet. There are three main types available: *hatcho miso*, made from soybeans and salt alone; *mugi miso*, made with fermented barley, soybeans, and salt; and *aka miso*, made from fermented rice, soybeans, and salt.

We have included a recipe for Miso Dressing and Marinade on page 64, but here also is a recipe for a popular miso soup.

Miso Soup with Onions and Spinach   Serves 2

1 tablespoon vegetable oil
2 scallions, thinly sliced
1 cup shredded fresh spinach

3 cups boiling Vegetable
  Stock (page 76)
1 tablespoon miso

1. In a large saucepan, heat the oil until hot. Add the scallions and spinach and sauté until they are wilted. Divide the mixture between 2 serving bowls.

2. Dilute the miso in a small amount of the broth and then return it to the broth. Stir well.

3. Pour the hot miso-broth mixture over the onions and spinach and serve immediately.

TEMPEH

Tempeh (pronounced *TEM-pay*) is also a fermented soybean product but, unlike miso, it is made without salt. Tempeh comes in white cakes or patties, bound by a dense white mold. The stage of fermentation will dictate the texture, aroma, and taste of the tempeh. Although pure soy tempeh is the most commonly available type, there are tempehs which combine soybeans with legumes, seeds, cereal grains, and coconut. Coconut-presscake tempeh should be avoided, as it occasionally becomes highly toxic. Since tempeh is much less common than tofu, you will probably only find tempeh at your natural foods store.

Basic Fried Tempeh   Serves 2 to 3

¼ cup water
¼ cup lemon juice
1 tablespoon soy sauce
½ teaspoon ground coriander

Juice from 1 clove garlic
6 ounces tempeh, cut
  into slices or cubes
Vegetable oil for deep-frying

1. Combine the water, lemon juice, soy sauce, coriander, and garlic juice in a mixing bowl.

2. Dip the tempeh slices into the mixture, then shake or pat with a paper towel to remove the excess moisture.

3. Heat the oil to 350 degrees and deep-fry the tempeh until golden brown — only a matter of minutes.

4. Serve simply fried, or use the fried tempeh slices as a basis for other dishes. Try dipping the tempeh cubes in your favorite fondue sauce or serve the slices with a variety of sauces.

TOFU

Tofu (pronounced *TOE-fu*), also known as soy cheese and bean curd, is made by solidifying soy milk. The amount of salt found in tofu depends primarily upon the type of coagulant used. It comes in both soft and firm cakes and is highly perishable, so cover it with water and refrigerate.

Sautéed Tofu and Mushrooms   Serves 6

3 tablespoons vegetable oil
1 pound fresh mushrooms, thinly sliced
6 scallions, cut into ½-inch lengths
Dash each of ground cumin, ground ginger, and white pepper
Juice from 1 clove garlic
2 teaspoons cornstarch
1 tablespoon water
2 cups Vegetable Stock (page 76)
24 cubes tofu, each 1 inch in size

Green Pasta Salad

1. Heat the oil in a skillet and add the mushrooms, scallions, spices, and garlic juice. Sauté until the mushrooms are limp.

2. Dissolve the cornstarch in the water and combine it with the stock.

3. Add the stock to the skillet. As the mixture starts to thicken, add the tofu cubes, stirring carefully.

4. Heat thoroughly, then serve.

Tofu-Cheese Rarebit   Serves 4

½ cup beer   1 tablespoon cornstarch
½ cup chopped tofu   Black pepper
Miso   Dry mustard
2 cups grated cheddar cheese

1. Combine the beer, tofu, and miso in a blender and purée.

2. Transfer the tofu mixture to a saucepan and heat.

3. Meanwhile, combine the remaining ingredients and add them to the tofu. Cook, stirring, until the cheese has melted and the sauce is of desired consistency.

4. Serve poured over whole-wheat toast, alfalfa sprouts, and tomato slices.

Tofu and Bean Sprout Omelette   Serves 4 to 6

6 tablespoons butter
½ pound mung bean sprouts
2 small onions, thinly sliced
1 stalk celery, thinly sliced
12 ounces tofu, cut into ½-inch cubes

3 large eggs
1½ tablespoons water
White pepper
Peanut Sauce (page 71)

1. In a skillet, melt 3 tablespoons of butter and add the sprouts, onions, and celery. Sauté for 5 minutes, then remove from the pan and set aside.

2. Place the tofu on paper toweling and let stand for 10 minutes to drain excess moisture. Meanwhile, combine the eggs, water, and pepper and blend well.

3. In a skillet, melt the remaining butter over medium heat, tilting the pan to coat the sides. Pour the egg mixture into the pan and reduce the heat to low. Cook the eggs, pushing them from the edge of the pan to the center, just until the eggs are slightly set on the bottom.

4. Spoon the sprout mixture and the tofu over the eggs and continue to cook over low heat, stirring the mixture lightly a few times until the tofu is hot.

5. Serve the omelette hot, with Peanut Sauce.

CHAPTER
9

Eggs, Cheese, and Pasta

EGGS, CHEESE, AND PASTA

Although almost everyone has made dishes that use eggs or cheese, we include these items here because they are such an important part of the vegetarian diet. Of course, not all vegetarians eat eggs, but for those who do, these recipes will be of interest.

Pasta has always been thought of in terms of Italian food, but it is really more than that. It is a very good source of protein, especially when combined with cheese. People are thinking up ever-increasing uses for this food, popular with young and old alike.

EGGS

Baked Eggs with Cheese   Serves 8

2 tablespoons butter
1½ cups grated mild cheese, such as American or colby cheese
¼ cup sliced green onions or scallions, greens included
8 large eggs
⅔ cup half-and-half

1. Preheat the oven to 350 degrees.

2. Coat the bottom and sides of an 8 × 8 × 2-inch baking dish with butter. Sprinkle half the cheese and all of the onions over the bottom.

3. Make 8 slight depressions in the cheese-onion layer. Break the eggs, 1 by 1, over the depressions, and slip the eggs into their nests.

4. Pour the half-and-half over the eggs, and then sprinkle with the remaining cheese.

5. Bake the dish until the eggs are set — about 20 to 25 minutes. Serve hot.

Roquefort and Apple Omelette

Serves 2 to 3

3 tablespoons butter
2 tart apples, peeled, cored, and sliced
5 large eggs
2 tablespoons milk
2 tablespoons grated Parmesan cheese
Black pepper
½ cup crumbled Roquefort cheese

1. In a skillet, melt 2 tablespoons of butter. Add the apple slices and sauté for 1 minute. Remove the apples from the skillet and set aside.

2. In a mixing bowl, combine the eggs, milk, Parmesan cheese, and pepper. Mix well.

3. Add the remaining butter to the skillet and heat until hot enough to sizzle a drop of water. Pour the egg mixture into the pan and cook quickly. With a fork, lift cooked portions of the egg mixture at the edges so that the liquid on top flows underneath. When the omelette is set, remove it from the heat (it should be moist and creamy on top).

4. Sprinkle the Roquefort cheese and half the sautéed apples on 1 side of the omelette. Fold the omelette in half. Transfer it to a warmed dish and garnish with the remaining apple slices. Serve immediately.

CHEESE

Baked Cheese-Olives   Serves 10 to 12

¼ pound cheddar cheese, finely grated
½ pound butter
1 cup all-purpose flour
¼ teaspoon cayenne pepper
20 to 24 small stuffed green olives, well drained

1. Preheat the oven to 400 degrees.

2. In a bowl, thoroughly cream together the cheese and butter. Add the flour and pepper, blending until smooth. Chill.

3. Pinch off small amounts of the dough and press it around each olive. Place the olives on a greased cookie sheet and bake for 12 minutes, or until brown.

4. Remove from the oven and serve as a hot hors d'oeuvre.

Cheese and Mushroom Balls

Serves 6 to 8

4 ounces blue cheese, crumbled
3 cups fresh bread crumbs
1 can (2½ ounces) sliced mushrooms,
    drained and finely chopped
2 tablespoons chopped green onions
    or scallions

½ teaspoon savory
¼ teaspoon black pepper
2 large eggs, lightly beaten
Vegetable oil for deep-frying

1. In a mixing bowl, combine the cheese, 2 cups of bread crumbs, mushrooms, onions, savory, pepper, and eggs. Mix well, then let stand for 10 minutes.

2. Shape the mixture into balls 1 inch in diameter. Roll the cheese balls in the remaining bread crumbs.

3. Heat the oil to 350 degrees and deep-fry the balls until golden.

4. Drain the cheese balls on paper towels, then serve as an hors d'oeuvre.

Roquefort Mushrooms

Serves 10 to 12

8 ounces Roquefort cheese
½ cup butter
¼ cup cognac

1 pound fresh medium-sized
    mushrooms, stems removed
    and caps reserved

1. In a bowl, combine the cheese, butter, and cognac. Fill the mushroom caps with this mixture.

2. Place the stuffed mushrooms on a lightly greased cookie sheet and broil for 3 to 4 minutes, at about 4 to 5 inches from the heat.

3. Remove from the broiler and serve the mushrooms as an hors d'oeuvre.

Parmesan Crowns   Serves 4

½ cup mayonnaise
¼ cup grated Parmesan cheese
¼ cup finely chopped green onion tops
Dash of soy sauce
12 rounds (1½ inches in diameter) whole-wheat bread, sliced thinly

1. Preheat the oven to 450 degrees.

2. Combine all the ingredients in a bowl, except the bread slices. Spread the mixture on the slices of bread.

3. Place the bread slices on a greased baking sheet and sprinkle with additional Parmesan cheese, if desired. Bake until the crowns are puffy and lightly browned — about 8 minutes.

4. Serve hot, as an hors d'oeuvre.

Cheese Soup   Serves 8

5 tablespoons butter
¾ cup shredded carrots
½ cup diced celery
1 cup minced onion
½ cup shredded, pared parsnips

¼ cup all-purpose flour
4 cups Vegetable Stock (page 76)
3 cups shredded extra-sharp
  cheddar cheese
2 cups half-and-half

1. In a saucepan, melt 2 tablespoons of butter and add the vegetables. Cook, covered, for 10 minutes.

2. Melt the remaining butter and add to vegetables. Sprinkle with the flour. Toss lightly but well.

3. Add the stock gradually, stirring constantly until the mixture is smooth.

4. Add the cheese and stir until melted.

5. Gradually add the half-and-half. Heat, but do not bring to a boil, then serve.

Note: The soup may be thickened with instant potato flakes instead of with flour.

Variation: If a smoother texture is desired, purée the cooked vegetables before adding the cheese and half-and-half.

Cheese-Onion Quiche   Serves 4 to 6

1 nine-inch pastry shell, partially prebaked and cooled
2 tablespoons butter
1 large onion, chopped
1½ cups shredded gouda cheese
¾ cup half-and-half
1 large egg
¼ teaspoon salt
¼ teaspoon dried oregano
¼ teaspoon caraway seeds

1. Preheat the oven to 350 degrees.

2. Melt the butter in a skillet and add the onion. Sauté until limp, then remove from the heat.

3. Sprinkle half of the cheese over the bottom of the pastry shell. Add the sautéed onion and the remainder of the cheese.

4. Combine the half-and-half, egg, salt, oregano, and caraway seeds in a small bowl. Pour the mixture into the pastry shell.

5. Bake until the filling is set — about 35 minutes. Let the quiche stand for 10 to 20 minutes before cutting it.

Spinach Quiche   Serves 4 to 6

1 nine-inch pastry shell, partially prebaked and cooled
2 cups shredded Swiss cheese
1 cup chopped fresh spinach
2 tablespoons all-purpose flour
1¼ cups half-and-half
3 large eggs, lightly beaten
¼ teaspoon salt
¼ teaspoon ground nutmeg

1. Preheat the oven to 325 degrees.

2. In a mixing bowl, combine the cheese, spinach, and flour. Spread the mixture over the bottom of the pastry shell.

3. Combine the remaining ingredients and pour the mixture over the cheese-spinach mixture. Bake for about 35 minutes, or until set.

4. Let the quiche set for 10 to 20 minutes before cutting it.

Egyptian Michoteta   Serves 4 to 6

¼ pound feta cheese
3 tablespoons olive oil
½ teaspoon dried oregano
1 tablespoon lemon juice
Black pepper
2 medium cucumbers, thinly sliced
2 large, mild onions, thinly sliced
Lettuce

1. Combine the cheese, oil, oregano, lemon juice, and pepper in a blender. Purée to make a smooth sauce.

2. Arrange the cucumber and onion slices on a bed of lettuce. Just before serving, pour the cheese sauce over the lettuce.

PASTA

Egg Noodles with Walnut Sauce   Serves 4 to 6

1 package (1 pound) egg noodles
1½ cups shelled walnuts
½ cup pine nuts (optional)
¾ cup heavy cream
2 tablespoons fresh bread crumbs

Juice from 1 clove garlic
¼ teaspoon dried marjoram
Black pepper
2 tablespoons butter

1. Cook the egg noodles according to the directions on the package. While the noodles are cooking, combine and grind the nuts in a blender.

2. Combine the cream, bread crumbs, garlic juice, marjoram, and pepper in a saucepan, then stir in the ground nuts. Heat the mixture over low heat, stirring constantly.

3. Drain the cooked noodles. Place them on a heated serving dish and toss them with the butter.

4. Add the warmed nut sauce, tossing until well blended. Serve immediately.

Pasta with Broccoli   Serves 4

1 package (1 pound) pasta spirals
4 cups fresh broccoli flowerets
½ cup olive oil
Juice from 1 clove garlic
⅛ teaspoon crushed dried red pepper
Grated Parmesan cheese

1. Bring salted water to a boil in a large pot, then add the broccoli and the pasta. Cook until both are done, then drain.

2. Meanwhile, heat the oil and seasonings together in a large skillet. When the pasta and broccoli are done, add them to the skillet. Toss well, and serve sprinkled with grated cheese.

Fettuccine with Green Beans   Serves 4

1 package (1 pound) fettuccine (narrow Italian noodles)
½ cup olive oil
1 can (16 ounces) french-style green beans, drained
Juice from 1 clove garlic
Cayenne pepper
Grated Parmesan and/or Romano cheese

1. Cook the fettuccine according to the directions on the package.

2. While the pasta is cooking, heat the oil in a large skillet. Add the beans, garlic juice, and pepper; heat thoroughly.

3. Drain the cooked fettuccine and add it to the skillet. Lift and toss the mixture until combined well. Transfer it to a heated serving dish, sprinkle with the cheese, and serve.

Fettuccine with Zucchini and Mushrooms   Serves 6

1 package (1 pound) fettuccine (narrow Italian noodles)
½ cup butter
½ pound fresh mushrooms, thinly sliced
1¼ pounds fresh zucchini, cut into julienne strips
1 cup heavy cream
¾ cup grated Parmesan cheese
½ cup chopped fresh parsley

1. Cook the fettuccine according to the directions on the package. Drain.

2. While the pasta is cooking, heat the butter in a large, deep skillet and sauté the mushrooms and zucchini over moderate heat for 2 minutes.

3. Add the cream to the skillet. Reduce the heat and simmer for 3 minutes.

4. Add the cooked and drained fettuccine, along with the cheese and parsley, to the skillet. Toss to mix well, and serve with additional grated cheese if desired.

Pasta with Roquefort   Serves 4

1 package (1 pound) spinach noodles
3 tablespoons butter
1 cup chopped onion
½ pound fresh mushrooms, sliced
3 tablespoons all-purpose flour
¾ cup crumbled Roquefort cheese
1 cup Vegetable Stock (page 76)
Dash of ground nutmeg
4 tablespoons heavy (whipping) cream

1. Cook the noodles according to the directions on the package. Drain.

2. Melt the butter in a skillet and sauté the onions and mushrooms for 5 minutes. Sprinkle with the flour and continue to cook for another 2 minutes.

3. Add the remaining ingredients and simmer, stirring constantly, until the sauce has thickened.

4. Toss the noodles with the sauce and top with additional crumbled Roquefort if desired.

Cold Pasta Salad   Serves 6

1 avocado, seeded, peeled, and cut into bite-sized chunks
⅔ cup Italian salad dressing
1 package (9 ounces) frozen artichoke hearts, cooked according to
    directions
½ pound small button mushrooms, or large mushrooms, quartered
½ cup sliced black olives
⅓ cup chopped anchovy filets (optional)
1 cup mayonnaise
Tabasco sauce or cayenne pepper
1 pound cooked thin spaghetti

1. Marinate the avocado chunks in ⅓ cup salad dressing.

2. Combine the artichoke hearts, mushrooms, and remaining dressing in
a large pot. Thoroughly warm the mixture, stirring occasionally.
Remove from the heat.

3. Add the remaining ingredients to the pot, including the marinated
avocado. Toss gently but well.

4. This salad may be served either at room temperature or thoroughly
chilled.

Green Pasta Salad Serves 6

¼ cup olive oil
½ cup chopped fresh parsley
¼ cup fresh basil
Juice from 1 clove garlic
Black pepper
1 cup Yogurt Mayonnaise (page 58)
3 scallions, sliced, including greens
1 package (12 ounces) small shell macaroni, cooked, drained, and cooled
1 tablespoon finely chopped fresh chives

1. Combine the oil, parsley, basil, and seasonings in a blender and purée to a paste.

2. Add the mayonnaise and the scallions to the paste. Blend to a pale green creamy sauce.

3. Toss the pasta with the sauce. Cover and refrigerate several hours or overnight. Garnish with chives before serving.

Yogurt and Yogurt Dishes

YOGURT AND YOGURT DISHES

Yogurt is something just about everyone knows quite well today. But although you might eat your yogurt regularly as a lunch or snack, there are many ways you can also use it in soups or main dishes. You'll find yogurt included in other recipes in this book, but here are a few special ones you might want to try. In addition, we give you a recipe for making your own yogurt — something you will find quite easy to do.

Yogurt is very versatile, offering a slightly tangy taste to hot or cold foods. It is important to remember, however, that yogurt will separate unattractively (though harmlessly) when heated unless it has been stabilized with cornstarch or flour (1 tablespoon for every 1 cup of yogurt) or egg (1 egg per cup of yogurt). If it does separate, just stir it back together.

Making your own yogurt is simplicity itself. All you need are milk and some friendly bacteria. Yogurt is milk coagulated and fermented by two types of benign bacteria. The coagulation is brought about by the action of *Lactobacillus bulgaricus*, while *Streptococcus thermophilus* ferments the milk sugar into lactic acid. This gentle acid curdles the protein in yogurt and acts as a preservative. Sometimes a third strain of bacteria, *Lactobacillus acidophilus*, is included in the yogurt culture.

Basic Plain Low-Fat Yogurt   Makes 1 quart

1⅔ cups instant nonfat dry milk powder
3¾ cups water
2 tablespoons fresh live yogurt (from your dairy case) or 1 package dried
   culture (from your natural foods store)

1. Thoroughly blend the water and the powdered milk. Bring the mixture to a boil; this will kill the bacteria in the milk that would otherwise render the bacteria in the starter ineffective.

2. Remove the milk from the heat and, stirring occasionally, allow the milk to cool to 112 degrees Fahrenheit. This is the ideal temperature for the yogurt bacilli to multiply. The bacteria will die if the temperature of the milk is over 120 degrees and will remain inactive if it is under 90 degrees.

3. Place the fresh or dried yogurt culture (called the starter) in your blender. Add the lukewarm milk and blend thoroughly.

4. Place the mixture into an electric yogurt maker or use a wide-mouth Thermos bottle. (Prewarm the Thermos by rinsing it with warm water; pour the lukewarm mixture in and seal.) Leave the yogurt undisturbed for about 6 hours or until the yogurt is set (it may take a bit longer if you have used a dried culture). Once the yogurt is firm, refrigerate it until it is chilled thoroughly. It is now ready for whatever use you intend.

Note: Maintaining the same temperature while the yogurt develops is important. Yogurt bacilli are very sensitive to temperature changes and it is mandatory that a steady temperature of approximately 112 degrees be maintained. Also, to ensure a continuous supply of yogurt, remember to reserve a small quantity from each batch to serve as the starter for your next batch.

Chilled Cucumber Soup   Serves 4

1 cup chilled Vegetable Stock (page 76)
1 cup plain yogurt
1 small cucumber, peeled, seeded, and cubed
White pepper
Chopped fresh chives

1. Purée all the ingredients in a blender except the chives.

2. Pour the mixture into a container and chill. When ready to serve, sprinkle with chives.

Note: If the soup separates as it chills, just give it a stir right before serving.

Chilled Tomato-Yogurt Soup   Serves 4

1 cup tomato sauce
5 scallions, chopped (reserve some of the tops for garnish)
Juice from 1 clove garlic
1 tablespoon Italian Seasoning (page 48)
1 tablespoon Curry Powder (page 48)
3 ounces dry vermouth
2½ cups Vegetable Stock (page 76)
1 cup plain yogurt

1. Combine all the ingredients except the yogurt. Simmer them in a covered pot for 20 minutes.

2. Purée the mixture if a smoother consistency is desired. Chill.

3. When ready to serve, stir in the yogurt and garnish with scallion greens.

Variation: This soup is also delicious served hot, but remember to add 1 tablespoon flour or cornstarch (or 1 egg) to the yogurt before heating to prevent curdling.

Yogurt Barley Soup   Serves 2

2 cups Vegetable Stock (page 76)
¼ cup uncooked barley
1 can (4 ounces) mushroom pieces, with liquid
1 large egg
2 cups plain yogurt
Fresh dill

1. Heat the stock and add the barley. Cover and simmer gently, stirring occasionally. Cook until tender — about 1 hour.

2. Add the mushrooms and mushroom liquid to the pot.

3. Blend the egg with the yogurt and slowly add this to the soup. Continue cooking, stirring often, until the soup is heated through.

4. Sprinkle the fresh dill on the top of the soup and serve.

Yogurt Quiche

Serves 4 to 6

1 nine-inch pastry shell, partially prebaked and cooled
1 tablespoon cornstarch
¼ cup milk
1 cup plain yogurt
3 large eggs
2 tablespoons finely sliced scallions
1 hot red pepper, finely chopped
¼ teaspoon black pepper
⅛ teaspoon ground nutmeg
1½ cups shredded mozzarella cheese
2 tablespoons grated Romano or Parmesan cheese

1. Preheat the oven to 375 degrees.

2. Dissolve the cornstarch in the milk.

3. Combine all the remaining ingredients except the Romano or Parmesan cheese, and then blend in the cornstarch mixture. Mix well.

4. Pour the mixture into the shell and sprinkle the top with the Romano or Parmesan cheese.

5. Bake for about 30 to 35 minutes, or until nicely browned. Let the quiche stand for 10 minutes before cutting it.

Yogurt Waffles   Makes 6 to 8 waffles

1 cup all-purpose flour
1 cup rolled oats or old-fashioned oatmeal
½ cup yellow cornmeal
4½ teaspoons baking powder
2 cups buttermilk
1 cup plain yogurt
¾ cup vegetable oil
2 large eggs

1. Combine the flour, oats, cornmeal, and baking powder in a large bowl. Blend well.

2. Add the buttermilk, yogurt, oil, and eggs and blend together with the dry mixture. Let the batter stand for 15 minutes.

3. Preheat the waffle iron, then pour the batter to cover about two-thirds of the griddle. Bake until steam has stopped escaping from the iron and the waffles are golden — about 3 to 4 minutes. Serve with syrup or jam.

CHAPTER
11

Fish, for the
Part-Time Vegetarian

FISH, FOR THE PART-TIME VEGETARIAN

Although this is primarily a vegetarian cookbook, some recipes using fish and shellfish have been included. Some people may choose to skip this chapter, if they like, but for a very large number of readers, fish and shellfish remain a viable food source. Fish is nutritious, delicious, and a good low-calorie alternative to meat.

There are lots of cookbooks around with tasty recipes for fish. This chapter makes no attempt to be comprehensive; these are just a few favorite uses for fish and shellfish. If you haven't switched over to a completely vegetarian diet, then perhaps some of these dishes will tempt you.

CAVIAR

Caviar Cucumbers   Serves 6

2 small cucumbers, pared but leaving narrow strips of peel
4 ounces cream cheese, at room temperature
¼ cup + 2 tablespoons sour cream
1 teaspoon chopped fresh dill
2 teaspoons minced onion
Salmon caviar

1. Cut the cucumbers lengthwise in half and scoop out the seeds. Cut
the halves into 2-inch pieces.

2. Combine the cream cheese, sour cream, dill, and onion in a bowl,
then spoon the mixture into the cucumber chunks.

3. Top with caviar, and serve as an appetizer.

Caviar Mushrooms   Serves 4

½ pound fresh mushrooms
¼ pound butter, softened
1 ounce lumpfish caviar

1. Preheat the oven to 325 degrees.

2. Remove the stems from the mushrooms. Reserve the caps and mince the stems.

3. Combine the minced stems with the butter and caviar.

4. Place the mushroom caps on a lightly greased baking sheet and fill each cap with the caviar mixture. Bake until the butter melts and then serve hot as an appetizer.

Carob-Dipped Strawberries

Caviar Potatoes   Serves 4 to 6

25 very tiny new or red bliss potatoes
1 jar (2 ounces) lumpfish roe or other caviar
1 cup sour cream
Chopped fresh chives

1. Preheat the oven to 375 degrees.

2. Bake the potatoes for about 30 minutes, or until they are done.

3. Slice a small piece from the bottoms of the potatoes so that they will sit steadily in a dish. Make a slip in the top of each potato and then scoop out a small amount of pulp.

4. Fill the hollow with ½ teaspoon of roe, then top with a dollop of sour cream and sprinkle with chives.

5. Serve warm, as an appetizer.

SHELLFISH

Hot Clam-Cheese Dip   Serves 10 to 12

1 can (7 ounces) minced clams, drained
1 jar (5 ounces) sharp cheddar cheese spread
¼ medium green pepper, minced
2 green onions or scallions, including green part, minced
3 dashes Tabasco sauce
Juice from 1 clove garlic

1. Combine all the ingredients in a saucepan and simmer for about 10 minutes, stirring constantly.

2. Serve hot, with tortilla chips.

Shrimp Dip   Serves 6 to 8

1 cup shelled and cooked shrimp
4 ounces cream cheese, at room temperature
¼ cup plain yogurt
1 tablespoon finely chopped onion
1 teaspoon Curry Powder (page 48)
Juice from 1 clove garlic

1. Combine the ingredients in a blender and purée.

2. Transfer the mixture to a serving bowl, cover, and chill overnight. Serve with crisp raw vegetables.

Clam-Zucchini Soup   Serves 4

3 tablespoons butter
1 medium onion, chopped
1 pound fresh zucchini, chopped
1 large carrot, peeled and chopped
2 medium potatoes, peeled and chopped
1½ cups Vegetable Stock (page 76)
1 tablespoon ground cumin
1 can (7 ounces) minced clams, with liquid
½ cup milk or light cream
Ground white pepper

1. In a heavy soup kettle, melt the butter and sauté the onion for 5 minutes.

2. Add the zucchini, carrot, potatoes, stock, and cumin to the kettle. Bring to a boil, then reduce the heat and simmer until the vegetables are just tender — about 15 minutes.

3. Purée the cooked mixture in a blender, then return the purée to the kettle. Add the remaining ingredients and reheat slowly. Serve hot.

Green Crab Soup   Serves 4

2 cups Vegetable Stock (page 76)
1 can (10½ ounces) condensed green pea soup
1 cup plain yogurt
1 tablespoon all-purpose flour
1 can (7 ounces) crabmeat, cleaned and flaked
2 tablespoons rum, brandy, or sherry
Black pepper
1 tablespoon chopped fresh chives

1. In a saucepan, combine the stock and the soup concentrate.

2. Meanwhile, combine the yogurt and the flour in a blender. Add to the stock.

3. Add the crabmeat, rum, and pepper to the soup and blend. Heat, but do not overcook.

4. Garnish with chives and serve hot.

Oyster and Spinach Soup

Serves 8 to 10

½ cup butter
½ cup finely chopped onion
3 cans (12 ounces) oysters, drained and chopped
Black pepper
Juice from 1 clove garlic
½ cup all-purpose flour
1½ quarts milk or half-and-half
2 cups Vegetable Stock (page 76)
2 packages (10 ounces) frozen spinach, thawed and puréed

1. In a saucepan, melt the butter and sauté the onion. Add the oysters and the seasonings. Cook until the oyster edges begin to curl.

2. Blend in the flour and cook until the mixture is bubbly. Gradually add the milk. Cook, stirring constantly, until the mixture is thickened.

3. Stir in the stock and the spinach, and heat thoroughly. Serve hot.

Broiled Scallops   Serves 4 to 6

2 pounds fresh or frozen scallops
¼ cup honey
¼ cup prepared mustard
1 teaspoon Curry Powder (page 48)
1 teaspoon lemon juice

1. Rinse the fresh scallops well in cold water, or thaw and rinse frozen
scallops. Place them in a baking pan.

2. In a small bowl, combine the remaining ingredients. Brush the
scallops with this sauce.

3. Broil the scallops approximately 4 inches from the heat source for 5
minutes, or until browned. Turn the scallops, brush with the
remaining sauce, and broil 5 minutes longer. Serve hot.

Shrimp Scampi   Serves 6 to 8

Vegetable oil for frying
3 pounds large shrimp, shelled but with tail left on
Black pepper
Juice from 1 clove garlic
½ cup finely chopped fresh parsley

1. In a heavy skillet, heat the oil until hot. Add the shrimp, pepper, and garlic juice and sauté the shrimp, stirring constantly, for about 5 minutes, or until done. Be careful not to let the shrimp stick to the pan.

2. Turn off the heat and add the parsley, then serve.

Crab Wontons   Serves 6 to 8

½ pound crabmeat, cleaned and chopped
½ pound cream cheese, at room temperature
½ teaspoon Spicy Soy Sauce (page 72)
Juice from 1 clove garlic
2 to 3 dozen wonton wrappers
1 egg yolk, lightly beaten
Vegetable oil for deep-frying
Chinese Hot Mustard Sauce (page 71)
Sweet and Sour Sauce (page 72)

1. In a bowl, combine the first 4 ingredients. Blend to a paste.

2. Place a heaping teaspoonful of paste on each wonton wrapper. Bring the four corners of the wrapper together at the top, moisten the edges with egg yolk, and pinch or twist them together gently to seal.

3. Heat the oil to 375 degrees. Add the wontons in batches and fry until golden — about 3 minutes. Remove each with a slotted spoon and drain on paper towels.

4. Serve the wontons with the sauces for dipping.

Shrimp in a Cheese Ring

Serves 4 to 6

CHEESE RING:

1 cup milk
¼ cup butter
1 cup all-purpose flour
4 large eggs + 1 egg white, lightly beaten
1 cup shredded sharp cheddar cheese
1 teaspoon prepared mustard
½ teaspoon black pepper

FILLING:

1 cup Vegetable Stock (page 76)
½ cup dry white wine
2 pounds shelled small shrimp
6 tablespoons butter
½ cup minced onion
3 tablespoons all-purpose flour
¼ cup chutney
¼ teaspoon black pepper
¼ cup grated Parmesan cheese

1. Prepare the ring the day before. In a medium-sized saucepan, bring the milk and butter to a boil, then remove from the heat.

2. Stir in the flour, then add the whole eggs, 1 at a time, beating in each one. Add the remaining ingredients except the egg white. Cook the mixture over low heat until the cheese melts.

3. Fit the mixture into a large ring mold, or shape it into a buttered 10-inch pie plate. Brush the dough with the egg white, then refrigerate, covered, overnight.

4. The next day, prepare the filling. Preheat the oven to 400 degrees.

5. Combine the stock and the wine in a saucepan and bring to a boil. Add the shrimp, reduce the heat, and simmer, uncovered, until the shrimp are cooked — no more than 4 minutes. Remove the shrimp with a slotted spoon and reserve both shrimp and broth.

6. In a saucepan, melt the butter and sauté the onion for 5 minutes. Sprinkle on the flour and stir, then add the reserved broth and simmer the mixture until it is smooth and thick — about 5 minutes. Remove from the heat, add the chutney, pepper, and the reserved shrimp.

7. Fill the ring with the shrimp mixture and sprinkle the top with Parmesan cheese.

8. Bake the ring until puffed and brown — about 40 to 45 minutes.

Crab in Cheese Pastries

Serves 8 to 10

PASTRY:

½ cup butter, softened
¼ cup cream cheese, softened
2 tablespoons heavy (whipping) cream
1¼ cups all-purpose flour

FILLING:

1 tablespoon butter
1 cup flaked crabmeat
1 scallion or shallot, finely chopped
1 tablespoon dry sherry
3 large eggs, lightly beaten
¾ cup milk
1 cup shredded swiss or gruyère cheese
¼ teaspoon black pepper

1. Preheat the oven to 400 degrees.

2. Prepare the pastry. In a bowl, beat together the butter and the cream cheese until smooth and creamy — about 3 minutes.

3. Add the cream, blending well, then fold in the flour gradually. Gather the dough into a firm ball.

4. Roll the dough ⅛ inch thick on a lightly floured surface. Cut 2-inch circles with a biscuit cutter, then press the circles into a greased set of muffin cups. Refrigerate the dough for 20 minutes.

5. Bake the pastries for 5 minutes. Cool before filling.

6. Prepare the filling. In a saucepan, melt the butter and sauté the crabmeat with the scallion for 1 minute.

7. Stir in the sherry and simmer an additional minute.

8. Combine the remaining ingredients and stir into the crab mixture.

9. Spoon the crab mixture by 2 tablespoonsful each into the pastry shells. Bake until the filling is set and the pastry is slightly puffy — about 20 minutes. Serve hot.

Clam Quiche in Wheat-Germ Pastry   Serves 4 to 6

PASTRY:

¾ cup wheat germ
½ cup whole-wheat flour
¼ teaspoon salt
¼ cup butter
1 large egg, lightly beaten

FILLING:

1 can (15 ounces) condensed New England Clam Chowder
4 large eggs, lightly beaten
½ cup finely chopped onion
2 teaspoons chopped fresh parsley
¼ teaspoon black pepper
1 can (6 ounces) evaporated milk
½ cup shredded mozzarella cheese

1. Preheat the oven to 450 degrees.

2. Prepare the pastry shell by combining the wheat germ, flour, and salt in a bowl. Cut in the butter until the mixture resembles coarse meal.

3. With a fork, blend in the egg. Roll out the dough on a floured surface and cut to fit a 9-inch baking pan. Press the dough against the bottom and sides of the pie pan and poke a series of holes in the bottom. Line the pastry shell with aluminum foil, then fill with weights.

4. Bake the pastry shell for 10 minutes, then allow to cool before filling. Reduce the oven temperature to 325.

5. Prepare the filling by combining in a bowl the chowder concentrate, eggs, onion, parsley, pepper, and evaporated milk.

6. Pour the mixture into the prepared shell and sprinkle the cheese on top. Bake for 35 minutes, or until the filling is set. Let it stand for 10 to 20 minutes, then cut and serve.

Scallop and Lemon Rice Salad   Serves 4

1 pound scallops, cut into bite-sized pieces if very large
1 cup dry white wine
1 small onion, sliced
½ teaspoon dried thyme leaves
1 bunch watercress, leaves only
4 cups cooked rice, cooled to room temperature
½ cup Lemon Yogurt Sauce I (page 74)

1. Place the scallops in a saucepan and add the wine, plus enough water to cover the scallops. Add the onion slices and the thyme. Simmer until the scallops are cooked — about 3 minutes. Drain.

2. Combine the scallops and onion slices with the watercress, rice, and sauce. Toss to mix thoroughly, then serve.

FISH

Fish Pâté   Makes 1 quart

1 cup finely diced carrots
1 cup shelled fresh peas
1 pound sole or flounder fillets, cut up
1 egg white
1 teaspoon salt
¼ teaspoon white pepper
⅛ teaspoon ground nutmeg
1 cup firmly packed chopped fresh spinach
1 cup heavy cream

1. Cook the carrots and peas in boiling water just until tender — not
more than a few minutes. Drain the vegetables, then rinse with cold
water.

2. Combine the fish, egg white, salt, pepper, nutmeg, and spinach
in a food processor and purée. Transfer the purée to a metal bowl and
refrigerate, covered, for 1 hour.

3. Preheat the oven to 375 degrees.

4. Add the heavy cream to the fish mixture, ¼ cup at a time, and beat
until the fish purée is fluffy.

5. Fold in the peas and carrots, then spoon the mixture into a buttered 1-quart loaf pan. Rap the pan sharply to expel any bubbles. Smooth the top of the pâté, then cover with a buttered sheet of waxed paper and then with heavy-duty foil.

6. Place the loaf pan into a deep-sided baking pan, adding enough water to the baking pan to reach halfway up the sides of the loaf. Bake for 40 minutes.

7. Transfer the loaf pan to a rack, remove the foil and the waxed paper, and let stand for 10 minutes.

8. Place a platter over the loaf pan, then invert them both. The pâté should now come out of its cooking pan and slide onto the platter. Blot up any liquid on the platter with paper towels.

9. Serve sliced with a thick white wine sauce or with a lobster sauce.

Fish with Rice Noodles in Broth   Serves 6

2 pounds whitefish, cut into thin slices
Spicy Soy Sauce (page 72)
1 pound rice noodles
6 cups Vegetable Stock (page 76)

1. Marinate the fish slices covered with Spicy Soy Sauce for 20 minutes.

2. Meanwhile, in a large bowl, soak the rice noodles in enough warm water to cover for 5 minutes; drain.

3. In a large kettle, combine the stock with 3 tablespoons of Spicy Soy Sauce (use some of the marinade). Bring the stock to a boil and add the noodles. Cook over moderate heat for 5 minutes. Remove from the heat.

4. Add the fish to the soup, stirring gently so as not to break the fish slices. Cover the kettle and let stand for 1 minute. Serve.

Salmon Bisque   Serves 4

6 tablespoons butter
1 tablespoon minced onion
5 tablespoons all-purpose flour
½ teaspoon chopped fresh dill
1¾ cups Vegetable Stock (page 76)
1 tablespoon tomato paste
½ cup dry white wine
1 can (7¾ ounces) salmon, with liquid but with bones and skin removed
1 cup plain yogurt

1. In a saucepan, melt the butter, then sauté the onion for 5 minutes.

2. Blend in the flour and the dill, then gradually stir in the broth and the tomato paste. Cook, stirring constantly, until the mixture is smooth and thick.

3. Add the wine and the salmon liquid. Cook over low heat for 10 minutes.

4. Meanwhile, mash the salmon and then add it to the sauce when ready. Purée the mixture, then return it to the saucepan.

5. Add the yogurt, heat, and then serve.

Variation: Retain some pieces of salmon to add to the soup if larger pieces are desired. It will give the soup a chunkier texture.

Salmon Loaf   Serves 4

1 can (8 ounces) salmon, boned, drained, and flaked
3 cups soft bread crumbs
3 large eggs, lightly beaten
½ cup milk
½ cup chopped onion
2 tablespoons chopped fresh parsley
½ teaspoon dried tarragon
6 sliced black olives
Black pepper
¼ cup lemon juice

1. Preheat the oven to 400 degrees.

2. In a large mixing bowl, combine all the ingredients. Pour the mixture into a greased loaf pan, then place the loaf pan in the oven. Bake for 25 minutes, or until done.

3. Serve the loaf hot, perhaps with a curry-flavored sauce.

CHAPTER
12

Desserts — The Finishing Touches

DESSERTS — THE FINISHING TOUCHES

Desserts don't need to be sugar-laden. And they also don't have to be time-consuming to prepare. Here are some easy, delicious recipes.

FRUIT DISHES

Apricot Whip   Serves 2

1 cup dried apricots
1 cup plain yogurt

Sugar or honey, if desired
1 tablespoon chopped nuts

1. Soak the apricots in hot water for 30 minutes. Drain.

2. Combine the apricots with the yogurt and sugar or honey, if desired, in a blender. Purée until smooth. Chill.

3. Serve chilled, sprinkled with nuts.

Curried Bananas with Yogurt   Serves 4

3 tablespoons butter
1 teaspoon Curry Powder (page 48)
4 medium bananas, peeled and halved lengthwise
⅓ cup plain yogurt, at room temperature
2 tablespoons toasted almond slivers

1. Melt the butter over moderate heat in a skillet. Add the curry
powder and cook for 2 to 3 minutes, stirring constantly.

2. Add the bananas and cook, uncovered, for 3 minutes. Turn the
bananas and cook an additional 2 minutes. Remove from the heat.

3. Spoon the yogurt over the bananas, sprinkle with almonds, and serve
at once.

Banana Delight   Serves 1 to 2

½ medium banana, peeled
1 tablespoon frozen orange juice concentrate
1 cup plain yogurt
Sugar or honey, if desired

1. Combine all the ingredients in a blender and purée.

2. Serve chilled.

Blueberry Cream   Serves 2

1 cup milk   1 tablespoon honey
1 cup plain yogurt   ½ teaspoon vanilla extract
1 cup fresh blueberries

1. Combine all the ingredients in a blender and purée.

2. Serve chilled.

Pears with Roquefort   Serves 4

1 can (29 ounces) halved pears, with syrup
½ cup Roquefort cheese, rolled into 8 balls
3 tablespoons cognac
Grated rind and juice of ½ lemon

1. Preheat the oven to 400 degrees.

2. Arrange the pears, cavity side up, in a baking dish. Place a cheese
ball in each cavity.

3. Combine the remaining ingredients and pour over the pears. Bake
until the pears are hot and the cheese has started to melt. Serve hot.

Carob Fluff   Serves 4 to 5

6 large eggs, separated
1 package (6 ounces) carob chips
2 tablespoons orange-flavored liqueur
Whipped cream
Finely ground almonds or almond slivers

1. Beat the egg yolks until they are thick and lemon-yellow.

2. Melt the carob chips in a double boiler, stirring to keep them from sticking. As soon as the carob is fully melted, mix it with the beaten yolks and stir until smooth. Add the liqueur.

3. Beat the egg whites until they are very stiff. Carefully fold the whites into the carob mixture.

4. Spoon the dessert into individual dishes and chill until set — at least 4 hours. When ready to serve, top with whipped cream and almonds.

Peanut Butter Apple   Serves 1

1 apple, cored   2 tablespoons peanut butter

1. Fill the cored apple with peanut butter.

2. Eat immediately and enjoy.

Poached Prunes in Wine

Serves 8

2 cups dry red wine, such as burgundy
½ cup granulated sugar
¼ cup cognac
3 tablespoons lemon juice
1 stick cinnamon
½ teaspoon ground ginger
1 pound pitted prunes
Chopped walnuts

1. Combine the wine, sugar, cognac, lemon juice, and spices in a saucepan. Bring to a gentle boil and simmer 5 minutes, stirring occasionally.

2. Add the prunes and continue to cook another 5 minutes. Remove the pan from the heat and let stand, covered, until cool. Then chill at least 3 hours.

3. Transfer the prunes and liquid to a serving dish and sprinkle with chopped nuts.

Note: These prunes can also be served over vanilla ice cream.

Gingered Yogurt   Serves 2

1 cup plain yogurt
6 tablespoons ginger marmalade or chopped crystallized ginger
4 teaspoons brown sugar
1 teaspoon lemon juice

1. Combine all the ingredients in a bowl and blend together well.

2. Chill, then serve.

Carob-Dipped Strawberries   Makes 2 pints

1 package (6 ounces) carob chips
½ cup butter
2 pints fresh strawberries, stems intact

1. In the top of a double-boiler, combine and melt the carob chips and butter.

2. Holding the strawberries by their stems, dip each berry into the carob-butter mixture to cover about three-quarters of the fruit. Put the strawberries, stem-side down, on a wire rack to set the coating.

Note: If your kitchen is too warm, you may need to place the rack in the refrigerator for the carob to set on the fruit.

Orange Strawberries   Makes 1 pint

(For this recipe you will need a plastic medical syringe and a large needle.)

¾ cup orange-flavored liqueur
¼ cup brandy
1 pint extra-large fresh strawberries

1. In a small bowl, combine the liqueur and the brandy.

2. Draw the syringe full of the above mixture. Insert the needle very close to the green hulls of the berries until the end of the needle reaches the cavity within. Gently but firmly push enough liquid into the cavity to fill it.

3. Place the berries attractively on a serving dish and serve.

FROZEN DESSERTS

Orange Sherbet   Makes 1½ pints

1 can (6 ounces) frozen orange juice concentrate
1½ cups milk
⅔ cup powdered milk
3 drops vanilla extract

1. Combine all the ingredients in a blender and mix thoroughly.

2. Pour the mixture into a suitable container and place in the freezer until firm.

3. Serve topped with fresh fruit and granola.

Coffee Ice Cream Supreme
Serves 4 to 6

1 banana, sliced
1 teaspoon lemon juice
2 tablespoons banana liqueur
¼ cups raisins
rum
1 package (1 quart) coffee ice cream
2 tablespoons scotch whiskey

1. Place the banana slices in a bowl and add the lemon juice and banana liqueur. Marinate for 30 minutes.

2. Meanwhile, place the raisins in a bowl with the rum to cover and marinate for 30 minutes.

3. Melt the ice cream and stir in the bananas, raisins, marinades, and whiskey. Return the mixture to the freezer to harden.

4. Serve this ice cream when firm, but not solid.

A SWEET MISCELLANY

Spirited Fruit

Brandy and/or wine   Dried fruits

1. Keep a jar of brandy and/or wine in the refrigerator.

2. Add dried fruits of your choice — apricots, raisins, dates, and so forth — when you have some leftover from a recipe. These flavored fruits will be ready at a moment's notice for desserts, curries, or for whatever other dishes that you may want to use them.

Fruit Syrup

Leftover fruit cooking liquids   Cornstarch
Canning syrups

1. Save the juice from canned or cooked fruits; freeze it if you like.

2. When ready to use, thicken the juice by adding a bit of cornstarch and cooking it until it reaches the desired consistency.

Note: A fruit syrup is a nice addition to cooked carrots.

Carob Syrup   Makes 1 cup

1 cup mild-flavored honey   ½ teaspoon vanilla extract
⅔ cup carob powder   Sprinkling of ground cinnamon

1. Heat the honey until warm enough to mix with carob powder easily. Add the carob, then add the remaining ingredients.

2. Cover the mixture and store as you would honey. Serve over ice cream or use to make carob milk (2 to 3 teaspoons carob syrup to 1 cup hot milk).

Apple Chutney   Makes 1 quart

3 green cooking apples, peeled, cored, and chopped
½ cup lime juice
3 stalks celery, thinly sliced
2 tablespoons ginger preserves
1 tablespoon chopped fresh chives
1 tablespoon chili sauce
½ cup raisins
¼ cup honey

1. In a large bowl, combine all the ingredients.

2. Transfer to a suitable container and chill. This uncooked chutney will keep in the refrigerator for about 1 week.

Spirited Marmalade

Makes 2½ cups

1 jar (16 ounces) orange or ginger marmalade
½ cup brandy or bourbon
Lemon juice as needed

1. Combine the marmalade and liquor in a saucepan. Simmer for 10 minutes over medium heat, stirring occasionally. If the mixture is too thick, thin it with a little lemon juice mixed with a small amount of water.

2. Store the marmalade in a lightly covered container in the refrigerator.

CHAPTER
13

Sandwiches for
Midday Meals

SANDWICHES FOR MIDDAY MEALS

You don't have to be a vegetarian to be depressed about the thought of yet another ham-and-cheese sandwich. Although the meat-bread combination is what everyone expects, sandwiches can be an exciting alternative. Whether you are a vegetarian or not, these following recipes may perk up your midday meal. Serving quantities are not given here for most of these recipes.

SPREADS

Chutney Nut-Wich

Toasted cashew nuts
Vegetable oil

Cheese Bread (page 297), toasted
Chutney

1. Place the nuts in a blender with just enough oil and blend to make a smooth paste.

2. Spread the toasted bread with the nut mixture. Add the chutney or serve alongside.

Cottage Cheese Delight

Cottage cheese
Chopped mixed nuts

Chopped dried apricots
Toasted raisin bread

1. Mix the cottage cheese with the nuts and apricots.

2. Spread the mixture on the toasted bread and serve.

Garden Sandwich

Dark bread slices
Butter mixed with a small amount of horseradish
Alfalfa sprouts
Cheese slices, preferably a mild cheese
Tomato slices
Avocado slices

1. Spread the bread slices with the butter-horseradish mixture.

2. Top with the sprouts, cheese, tomato, and avocado.

Crunchy Peanut Butter Sandwich

Raisin bread slices
Peanut butter

Sliced medium banana
Toasted sunflower seeds

1. Spread the bread slices with the peanut butter.

2. Add the slices of banana to the peanut butter and top with the sunflower seeds.

GRILLED SANDWICHES

Grilled Mushrooms and Cheese

Butter
Sliced fresh mushrooms
Rye bread slices
Slices of mild cheese, such as American
Alfalfa sprouts

1. Quickly melt the butter in a skillet and sauté the mushroom slices.

2. Place the mushrooms on top of the bread slices and then cover with the cheese slices.

3. Grill the sandwiches in a skillet until the cheese melts and the bread is toasted.

4. Top the sandwiches with sprouts and eat.

Grilled Tuna with Cheese

Whole-wheat bread slices
Prepared mustard
Tuna salad or plain tuna

Slices of mild cheese,
    such as American
Butter

1. Spread the bread slices with mustard. Make a sandwich of the tuna and the cheese.

2. Melt the butter and grill the sandwiches until the cheese melts and the bread is golden.

Open-Faced Chili Sandwich

Toasted dark bread
Chili, meatless or otherwise
Sliced green olives

Shredded sharp cheddar cheese
Plain yogurt or sour cream

1. Place the bread slices in an ovenproof dish. Top with the chili and the olive slices.

2. Sprinkle the sandwiches with cheese and broil them until the cheese melts.

3. Remove the dish from the broiler and add a dollop of yogurt or sour cream to the chili.

Broiled Eggplant Sandwich

Eggplant slices, partially peeled
Vegetable oil
Thick slices of dark bread
Garlic Butter (page 53)

Alfalfa sprouts
Black pepper
Mozzarella cheese, grated

1. Brush the eggplant slices with the oil and broil them on both sides.

2. Spread the bread with the garlic butter (toast the bread first if crispness is desired).

3. Top the bread slices with the sprouts, the cooked eggplant, and the pepper. Cover with the cheese.

4. Place the sandwiches in the broiler and grill until the cheese melts. Remove and serve.

Nachos Sandwich

Tortillas
Green chili relish
Minced onion
Minced tomato
Shredded mozzarella or cheddar cheese

1. Fry or toast the tortillas until crisp.

2. Place the tortillas on a baking sheet.

3. In a mixing bowl, combine the relish, onion, and tomato. Spoon the relish mixture onto the tortillas, and then sprinkle the cheese on top.

4. Broil the tortillas until the cheese melts. Serve hot.

Vegetable-topped Tortillas   Serves 4

1 medium zucchini, thinly sliced
1 medium onion, chopped
1 can (4 ounces) sliced mushrooms, with liquid
¼ cup chopped celery
2 tablespoons chopped sweet green pepper
4 corn tortillas
2 tablespoons vegetable oil
1 cup shredded cheddar cheese
½ cup sour cream
1 medium tomato, chopped
Chili sauce

1. In a saucepan, combine the zucchini, onion, mushrooms, celery, and green pepper. Cover and simmer until the vegetables are tender-crisp — about 10 minutes. Drain well.

2. Heat the oil and fry the tortillas until they are crisp. Drain on a paper towel.

3. Preheat the oven to 350 degrees.

4. Place the tortillas on a baking sheet. Top each with an equal amount of the vegetable mixture, then sprinkle with the cheese.

5. Bake until the cheese melts, then remove from the oven and top with a dollop of sour cream, bits of tomato, and some chili sauce. Serve immediately.

Pocket Sandwich

Pocket Bread (page 295) Alfalfa sprouts
Tabbouleh (page 96)

1. Briefly heat the bread in the oven until it puffs up.

2. Slice the bread to expose the pocket. Fill with the tabbouleh and the sprouts.

Note: Other ideas for pocket sandwiches include using leftover patties or loaf slices.

CHAPTER
14

Snacks and Special Treats

SNACKS AND SPECIAL TREATS

We generally think of snacks as "junk food," but since they are such a part of the American diet, it is hard to avoid them. Instead of eating the usual, store-bought fare, why not try some of these more healthful treats?

NUTS AND CHIPS

Curried Cashews   Makes 2 cups

¼ cup butter
2 cups cashew nuts
1 to 2 tablespoons Curry Powder (page 48)

1. Melt the butter over low heat in a large skillet, then sauté the cashews until they are browned.

2. Add the curry powder and continue to cook, stirring, for about 5 minutes more.

3. Drain the cashews on absorbent toweling, and allow to cool. Store in an airtight container.

Toasted Pecans or Mixed Nuts   Makes 2 cups

¼ cup butter
2 cups pecan halves, or a mixture of nuts
Salt

1. Preheat the oven to 325 degrees.

2. Melt the butter in a skillet, then add the nuts. Toss the nuts to coat them with the butter.

3. Transfer the nuts to a cookie sheet and bake until the nuts are browned on both sides.

4. Sprinkle the toasted nuts with salt, and allow to cool. Store in an airtight container.

Soy Nuts   Makes 6 cups

3 cups dried soybeans   ½ cup vegetable oil
5 cups water   Aromatic Salt (page 47)

1. Combine the soybeans and water in a bowl. Soak overnight in the refrigerator.

2. Place the soybeans and soaking water in a pot and bring to a boil, adding more water if necessary. Reduce the heat and simmer for 15 minutes — just enough to soften the beans. Skim off the foam and hulls that float to the surface.

3. Drain the soybeans in a colander. Spread them on an absorbent flat surface to dry.

4. Heat ¼ cup of oil in a large skillet. Add half the dried beans and sauté until golden brown, stirring frequently. Remove and drain. Repeat with the remaining oil and soybeans.

5. Lightly sprinkle the salt over the cooked beans. Serve as a garnish or snack.

Roasted Sunflower Seeds   Makes 2 cups

2 cups hulled sunflower seeds
1 tablespoon melted butter
1 teaspoon Spicy Soy Sauce (page 72) or Worcestershire sauce
Juice from 1 clove garlic

1. Preheat the oven to 325 degrees.

2. In a mixing bowl, combine all the ingredients and mix well.

3. Place the seeds in a shallow baking pan and toast in the oven for 30 minutes. Stir the seeds occasionally as the seeds turn golden and become crunchy. Store in an airtight container.

Cheesies

Makes 4 to 5 dozen

½ pound sharp cheddar cheese, grated
½ cup butter
½ teaspoon salt
1¼ cups whole-wheat flour
⅛ teaspoon dry mustard

1. Combine all the ingredients in a mixing bowl. Blend until smooth.

2. Shape the dough into a roll, wrap in waxed paper, and chill until firm.

3. Preheat the oven to 350 degrees.

4. Slice the dough to the desired thickness and place the slices on a greased cookie sheet. Bake until lightly browned — about 10 minutes.

Variation: Before baking the crackers, brush the cut rounds with beaten egg white and then sprinkle them with sesame seeds or paprika.

Golden Bowties   Makes 8 cups

1 package (1 pound) bowtie pasta   Salt
Vegetable oil for deep-frying   Seasonings of your choice

1. Cook the bowties according to the directions on the package, just
until the pasta is *al dente*. Drain and separate on paper towels.

2. Heat the oil in a large pot. When the pasta is completely dry,
deep-fry the bowties until crisp and golden.

3. Drain the bowties and season with salt and other seasonings to taste.
Store in a tightly closed container and use as a snack or garnish.

Eggplant Chips   Makes 2 dozen

1 small eggplant, peeled and cut into paper-thin slices
Vegetable oil for deep-frying

1. Drain the eggplant on paper toweling.

2. Heat the oil in a large pot to 375 degrees. Drop the eggplant slices
into the oil and fry until golden.

3. Drain the chips on paper towels, and season to taste with salt or
other flavorings.

Potato Chips   Makes 4 dozen

¼ cup butter
4 large potatoes, unpeeled and thinly sliced
Dash of onion salt

1. Preheat the oven to 425 degrees.

2. Melt the butter.

3. Arrange the potato slices, 1 layer deep, on a greased cookie sheet. Brush with the melted butter and then sprinkle with onion salt.

4. Bake the potatoes until they just begin to brown — about 45 minutes. Allow to cool, then store in an airtight container.

Potato Peel Crisps

Makes 2 cups

2 cups peels from baked, raw, or boiled potatoes
2 tablespoons butter
Salt and black pepper

1. Preheat the oven to 450 degrees.

2. Cut the potato peels into 3 × 4-inch strips. Arrange the strips in a single layer in a greased baking dish.

3. Dot the peels with butter and then sprinkle with salt and pepper. Bake for 5 to 25 minutes, or until they are very crisp.

Note: The wide difference in baking time is dependent upon whether you use cooked or raw potato peels. Peels from baked potatoes will cook in 5 to 7 minutes; from boiled potatoes, in 20 to 25 minutes; and raw peels, 15 to 20 minutes.

SWEET TREATS

Many kinds of snack combinations can be made when you combine dried fruits and nuts or seeds. These ingredients make healthful, tasty snacks for youngsters. Try the following combinations:

1. shelled and lightly salted sunflower seeds and raisins
2. walnuts, dates, dried apricots, and pumpkin seeds
3. peanuts, cashews, and chopped dried peaches

Apple Snack   Makes 4 cups

8 medium apples, peeled, cored, and halved

1. Preheat the oven to 225 degrees.

2. Shred the apples coarsely and place the shreds on a buttered cookie sheet.

3. Bake the apples until they are dry, then remove from the cookie sheet with a pancake turner and break into pieces. Store in an airtight container.

Peanut Butter Balls
Makes 2 dozen

1 cup Granola (page 281)
½ cup raisins

1 to 2 cups peanut butter

1. In a mixing bowl, combine the granola and the raisins.

2. Add enough peanut butter to make a stiff but not crumbly mixture. Roll the mixture into little balls about 1 inch in diameter and store in a covered container in the refrigerator.

Nut Balls
Makes 3 dozen

1 cup black walnuts
¼ cup hulled sunflower seeds
¼ cup sesame seeds
¼ cup tahini or butter

¼ cup honey
¼ cup crunchy peanut butter
1 cup carob chips

1. Grind the walnuts, sunflower seeds, and sesame seeds together.

2. Place the nut-seed mixture in a bowl and add the tahini, honey, and peanut butter. Blend well.

3. Form the dough into balls about 1 inch in diameter. Roll each ball in the carob chips, and then lay the balls on a cookie sheet in a single layer. Chill until firm.

Sesame Seed Fingers

Makes 4 dozen

4 large eggs
¾ cup granulated sugar
2½ teaspoons baking powder
½ cup vegetable oil
3 cups whole-wheat pastry flour
Toasted sesame seeds

1. Preheat the oven to 350 degrees.

2. Beat 3 of the eggs until frothy, then gradually add the sugar and baking powder. Beat for 3 minutes.

3. Add the vegetable oil to the egg mixture and beat for 1 minute more.

4. Add the flour, ½ cup at a time, beating well after each to incorporate.

5. Turn the dough onto a floured surface and shape into rolls 1 inch in diameter. Brush off any excess flour, and then cut the rolls into 3-inch-long fingers.

6. Place the fingers on a greased cookie sheet and brush them with the remaining egg, lightly beaten. Sprinkle with sesame seeds.

7. Bake the sesame fingers until golden — about 15 to 17 minutes, then transfer to a rack to cool. Store in an airtight container.

Granola (Basic Recipe)

Makes 4½ cups

3½ cups rolled oats
1 cup bran buds
½ cup brown sugar

½ cup vegetable oil
½ teaspoon salt
1 teaspoon vanilla extract

1. Preheat the oven to 300 degrees.

2. In a bowl, combine the oats, bran, and brown sugar. Add the oil, salt, and vanilla, stirring well.

3. Spread the mixture in a shallow baking pan and toast for 30 minutes, stirring after the first 15 minutes.

4. Remove the granola from the oven and cool thoroughly before storing in a covered container. Serve either as a breakfast cereal or an anytime snack.

Note: Granola is basically a combination of toasted grains and ground seeds. To this mixture is added any number of goodies: chopped nuts, raisins, whole seeds, honey, or syrup. It can be fortified easily with powdered milk, brewer's yeast, or wheat germ.

My Granola

Makes 6 cups

3½ cups rolled oats
1 cup bran buds
½ cup hulled sunflower seeds
1 cup chopped cashews
¼ cup tahini, thinned with vegetable oil if necessary
½ teaspoon salt
1 teaspoon vanilla extract
1 teaspoon ground cinnamon
1 cup honey
1 cup diced dried apricots, or any combination of dried fruits

1. Preheat the oven to 300 degrees.

2. Combine the oats, bran, sunflower seeds, and nuts in a bowl. Add the tahini, salt, extract, cinnamon, and honey and mix well.

3. Spread the mixture in a shallow baking pan and toast for 30 minutes, stirring after the first 15 minutes.

4. Remove the pan from the oven and toss immediately with the apricots to prevent the mixture from sticking together in lumps. When cooled, store in a covered container.

BEVERAGE SNACKS

A meal-in-a-glass, these drinks offer a nutritional storehouse with a minimum of effort. Ideal for the family on the go, they are also an interestingly different taste treat.

Virgin Mary   Serves 1

1 cup tomato juice
½ cup clam juice
Dash of Tabasco sauce or pepper

1. Combine the ingredients in a glass and mix well.

2. Serve hot or cold.

Creamy Tomato Cocktail   Serves 1

¼ cup cottage cheese   Black pepper
1 cup tomato juice

1. Combine the ingredients in the container of a blender.

2. Blend until the mixture is smooth, then chill and serve.

Chilled Onion Soup   Serves 1

½ cup onion soup (either canned or made from an instant mix)
1 cup buttermilk

1. Combine the ingredients in a tall glass and mix well.

2. Chill and serve.

Summertime Soup   Serves 1

1 teaspoon vegetable stock concentrate or bouillon cube, broken up
¼ cup boiling water
¼ medium cucumber, peeled and seeded
½ small tomato, peeled and seeded
1 teaspoon dehydrated onion flakes, plumped in water and drained
½ cup plain yogurt

1. Dissolve the vegetable concentrate or bouillon cube in the hot water, then allow to cool.

2. Combine the vegetable stock with all the remaining ingredients in a blender. Purée thoroughly.

3. Chill or serve at room temperature.

Pink Buttermilk

Serves 1

½ cup heated tomato juice
½ teaspoon vegetable bouillon granules
1 cup buttermilk

1. Dissolve the bouillon granules in the tomato juice. Place mixture in the refrigerator.

2. When cool, blend in the buttermilk and serve chilled or over ice.

Tiger's Milk Shake

Serves 1

1 cup chilled orange juice
2 tablespoons Tiger's Milk powder
1 tablespoon papaya syrup concentrate

1. Combine the ingredients in a glass and mix well.

2. Chill and serve.

Cafe au Chocolat   Serves 1

½ cup plain yogurt
½ cup chocolate ice cream
1 teaspoon instant coffee powder

1. Combine the ingredients in a blender and mix until smooth.

2. Chill and serve.

Apple Milk   Serves 1

½ cup milk
½ cup apple juice

1. Combine the ingredients in a glass and mix well.

2. Chill and serve.

Frozen Daiquiri

Serves 1

½ medium banana, peeled
½ cup apple juice
½ cup orange juice
1 tablespoon lime or lemon juice
3 ice cubes

1. Place all ingredients in a blender and purée.

2. Serve and enjoy.

Orange Shake

Serves 1

1 cup chilled orange juice
¼ cup powdered milk
⅛ teaspoon vanilla extract

½ teaspoon honey (optional)
3 ice cubes

1. Combine all the ingredients in a blender and purée.

2. Serve immediately.

Variation: Omit the ice cubes and add 1 large egg.

Three-Fruit Drink   Serves 1

½ cup orange juice   Few slices canned peaches
½ banana, peeled   ½ cup milk

1. Combine the ingredients in a blender and purée.

2. Chill and serve.

Basic Loaf, Corn Muffins, Carob Chip Cookies

CHAPTER

15

Bread, Biscuits, and Other Baked Goods

BREAD, BISCUITS, AND OTHER BAKED GOODS

The convenience of store-bought bakery products will never be able to replace the delicious aroma and taste of freshly baked goods. Unfortunately, bread-making is seen by many as requiring almost mystical powers. Not so! Dive in, give it a try, and see for yourself.

SOME BASIC INFORMATION

Ingredients: Flour should always be sifted for proper measurement. The coarser wheats are difficult to sift, however, and should be placed in a measuring cup in a series of large spoonfuls to prevent packing. Keep whole-wheat, bean, or nut flours in the refrigerator or freezer to keep them from becoming rancid.

The oils and fats in baked goods provide flavor and softness, but most can be used interchangeably. Sugars add flavor and crispness and aid browning. Granulated, light or dark brown sugar, or raw sugar may be used interchangeably.

Baking: Pans should never be greased with oil because the dough will absorb the oil and will stick to the pan. Instead, use a solid shortening.

Reheating: To freshen slightly stale baked products, place them in a paper bag, moisten the bag with water, and place them in a 350-degree oven until the bag is dry.

Freezing: To freeze baked products, first let them cool thoroughly. Properly wrapped, they should last up to 6 months. To use them, thaw them, while they are still wrapped, in a preheated 300-degree oven for 30 minutes, or until softened.

YEAST BREADS

Basic Loaf   Makes 2 loaves

3 cups warm water
3 cakes or packages of yeast
¼ cup granulated sugar or honey
9 to 10 cups flour of your choice
5 teaspoons salt
5 tablespoons oil

1. Combine the water, yeast, and sugar. Stir until the yeast is dissolved.

2. Add half the flour and all the salt. Beat until the batter is smooth. Add the remaining flour and blend well.

3. Pour the oil over the dough and knead in the bowl for no more than 2 to 3 minutes. The dough will absorb the oil. Cover the bowl and let the dough rise until doubled in bulk — about 45 minutes.

4. Punch down the dough and turn it onto a lightly floured board. Knead it lightly, then shape it into 2 loaves and place in buttered loaf pans. Cover and let rise again until doubled — about 30 minutes.

5. Preheat the oven to 400 degrees.

6. Bake the loaves until done — about 30 minutes. Cool.

Note: When using low-gluten flour, do not include more than one-third low-gluten wheat flour to two-thirds of a high-gluten flour. These low-gluten flours (rye, oats, corn, rice, barley, buckwheat, dried bean, and nuts) do not contain enough of the stretchy component of gluten to hold a bread together without crumbling.

Wheat Germ-Bran Bread   Makes 2 loaves

1 cup milk, scalded
1 cup water
6 tablespoons honey
6 tablespoons vegetable oil
1 tablespoon salt
2 large eggs
2 cakes or packages yeast
¼ cup warm water
½ cup bran buds
½ cup wheat germ
½ cup whole-wheat flour
4 to 5 cups all-purpose flour

1. Combine the first 6 ingredients; blend well.

2. Dissolve the yeast in the warm water; add it to the milk mixture. Stir in the remaining ingredients, adding just enough of the white flour to make a soft dough.

3. Turn the dough onto a floured surface and knead until it is smooth and elastic — about 10 minutes. Place the dough in a greased bowl, turning to grease the top. Cover with a damp towel, and let rise until doubled in bulk — about 1½ to 2 hours.

4. Divide the dough in half and place it on a floured surface. Roll each half into an 8 × 18-inch rectangle. Roll up, beginning at narrow edge, and press firmly into shape to eliminate air pockets. Pinch the seams and ends together and place dough, seam side down, in well-greased loaf pans. Cover and let rise until doubled in size.

5. Preheat the oven to 350 degrees and bake the loaves until they sound hollow when tapped — about 30 minutes. Remove from the pans and cool on wire racks.

Rye and Walnut Bread   Makes 2 round loaves

2 cakes or packages yeast
1¾ cups warm water
2¼ cups whole-wheat flour
2 cups white hard-wheat flour
1¼ cups rye flour
1 cup milk
⅓ cup oil (walnut oil, if possible)
2 teaspoons salt
⅔ cup coarsely chopped walnuts

1. Combine the yeast with ½ cup warm water. Let stand until bubbly — about 10 minutes.

2. Stir in the remaining ingredients except the walnuts and mix well. Transfer the dough to a floured surface and knead, adding additional white flour if the dough seems too sticky. Knead until smooth — about 8 to 10 minutes.

3. Form the dough into a ball, transfer it to a bowl greased with walnut oil, and turn the ball to coat it with the oil. Cover the dough with plastic wrap and let it rise until it has doubled in bulk — about 1 hour, 30 minutes.

4. Punch down the dough and knead in the walnuts. Halve the dough, forming each into a round loaf, and then put loaves, several inches apart, on a baking sheet sprinkled with cornmeal. Let the dough rise, uncovered, until almost double in bulk — about 40 minutes.

5. Preheat the oven to 400 degrees. Just before baking the loaves, cut 3 crescent-shaped slashes in the tops of each loaf with a very sharp knife or razor. Brush the loaves with water, then bake them for 5 minutes.

6. Brush the loaves again with water and bake them until they sound hollow when tapped on the bottom — approximately 40 minutes. Transfer the loaves to a rack to cool.

Pocket (Pita) Bread

Makes 6 flat loaves

1 cake or package yeast
1¼ cups warm water
Pinch of granulated sugar
1¾ cups all-purpose flour

1¼ cups whole-wheat flour
¼ cup olive oil
2 teaspoons salt
6 tablespoons sesame seeds

1. In a small bowl, dissolve the yeast and sugar in ¼ cup water. Let stand for 10 minutes.

2. In a large bowl, combine the remaining ingredients, except the sesame seeds. When the yeast mixture is ready, add it to this mixture. Stir the batter until a ball of dough is formed.

3. Turn the dough onto a floured surface. Knead, adding more flour if necessary, until the dough is smooth and satiny — about 10 minutes.

4. Divide the dough into 6 balls. Flatten the balls into ¼-inch-thick rounds. Cover the rounds with a towel and let them rise in a warm place for 45 minutes. Make sure there are no creases in the flattened dough or it will not rise properly.

5. Preheat the oven to 500 degrees.

6. Transfer the rounds to a baking sheet sprinkled with cornmeal. Sprinkle each round with 1 tablespoon sesame seeds. Bake the loaves for 12 to 15 minutes, or until puffed and golden. Place the loaves immediately into a covered pan to cool. (This allows the trapped steam to release of its own accord and keeps the bread from becoming hard.)

Note: This bread freezes especially nicely and can be reheated easily.

Cheese Bread

Makes 3 loaves

4 cakes or packages yeast
3 cups lukewarm water
¼ cup granulated sugar
1 tablespoon salt
4 large eggs
10 cups all-purpose flour
4 cups grated sharp cheddar cheese
⅓ cup caraway seeds
Softened butter

1. Dissolve the yeast in water.

2. In a large mixing bowl, add the yeast, sugar, salt, eggs, and 5 cups of flour. Beat until the dough is smooth — about 2 minutes.

3. Add the remaining ingredients except butter and blend thoroughly. Cover and let rise until the dough has doubled in bulk — about 30 minutes.

4. Stir down the dough and pour it into 3 greased loaf pans. Cover and let rise again, until the dough reaches the tops of the pans.

5. Preheat the oven to 375 degrees.

6. Bake the loaves for 1 hour, then turn them out onto a wire rack. Brush them with butter and allow them to cool before slicing.

BISCUITS

Best Biscuits Yet

Makes 1 dozen

2 cups all-purpose flour
3 teaspoons baking powder
½ teaspoon salt

¼ cup butter
⅓ cup milk
2 large eggs

1. Preheat the oven to 450 degrees.

2. In a large mixing bowl, combine the flour, baking powder, and salt. Cut in the butter and mix well. The mixture should develop to the consistency of coarse cornmeal.

3. In a separate bowl, combine the milk and eggs, then add this to the larger bowl.

4. Turn the dough onto a floured board and knead it lightly — no more than 10 times. Roll the dough to a thickness of ½ inch. Cut the biscuits in 2-inch rounds and bake them on an ungreased cookie sheet for 12 to 15 minutes.

Note: For crusty biscuits, roll the dough thinner and cut the biscuits smaller; place them farther apart on the sheet. For flaky biscuits, roll the dough thicker, cut the rounds larger, and place them closer together.

Herbed Cocktail Biscuits   Makes 4 dozen

1¼ cups grated Parmesan cheese
1 cup all-purpose flour
½ cup butter
¾ teaspoon dried marjoram
¾ teaspoon dried oregano
¾ teaspoon chopped fresh basil
½ teaspoon Worcestershire sauce
2 to 3 tablespoons dry white wine

1. In a bowl, combine the cheese, flour, butter, and herbs. Blend until the mixture resembles coarse meal.

2. Add the Worcestershire sauce and just enough wine to form the dough into a ball. Roll the dough into a 1½-inch-thick cylinder, then wrap it in plastic wrap and chill until firm — about 1 hour.

3. Preheat the oven to 400 degrees.

4. Slice the dough crosswise into ¼-inch-thick slices. Arrange the slices ½ inch apart on a baking sheet and bake until lightly browned — about 12 to 15 minutes.

5. Transfer the biscuits to a rack to cool. Store loosely covered until ready to serve.

Whole-Wheat—Onion Biscuits   Makes 1 dozen

2 cups whole-wheat flour
3 teaspoons baking powder
½ teaspoon salt
¼ cup butter

⅓ cup milk
2 large eggs
2 cups minced onions

1. Preheat the oven to 375 degrees.

2. In a bowl, combine the flour, baking powder, and salt. Cut in the butter and mix to a consistency of coarse meal.

3. In another bowl, combine the milk with the eggs and onions. Add this to the dry mixture and add additional milk if necessary to hold the dough together.

4. Turn the dough onto a floured board and knead it lightly. Roll it out to a thickness of ¼ inch, then cut into 2-inch rounds.

5. Place the rounds on a greased baking sheet and bake for 15 to 20 minutes.

MUFFINS

Corn Muffins   Makes 1 dozen

1½ cups all-purpose flour
⅔ cup yellow cornmeal
4 teaspoons granulated sugar
1 tablespoon baking powder
½ teaspoon baking soda
1½ teaspoon salt
½ teaspoon dried sage
2 large eggs, lightly beaten
1 cup buttermilk
¼ cup butter, melted and cooled
1 cup raw corn or canned corn, drained

1. Preheat the oven to 425 degrees.

2. In a bowl, combine the flour, cornmeal, sugar, baking powder, baking soda, salt, and sage.

3. In another bowl, combine the remaining ingredients. Add this to the dry mixture.

4. Pour the batter into a well-greased muffin tin and bake until puffed and golden — about 25 to 30 minutes.

Yogurt-Wheat Germ Muffins   Makes 1 dozen

1 cup whole-wheat flour
¾ cup wheat germ
3 tablespoons brown sugar
½ teaspoon baking powder
¼ teaspoon baking soda
½ teaspoon salt
1 large egg, lightly beaten
1 cup plain yogurt
6 tablespoons butter, melted and cooled
Granulated sugar (optional)

1. Preheat the oven to 375 degrees.

2. In a mixing bowl, combine the flour, wheat germ, brown sugar, baking powder, soda, and salt.

3. Add the egg, yogurt, and butter, stirring just enough to moisten the dry ingredients.

4. Spoon the batter into a well-greased muffin tin. Sprinkle lightly with sugar and bake until done — about 30 to 35 minutes.

Bran Muffins   Makes 3 dozen

⅔ cup butter
1¼ cups granulated sugar
4 large eggs
3 cups all-purpose flour
1 tablespoon baking soda
2 teaspoons salt
1 cup warm water
4 cups bran flakes
2½ cups buttermilk

1. Preheat the oven to 375 degrees.

2. In a large bowl, cream together the butter and sugar. Add the eggs, one at a time, and blend well.

3. In a small bowl, combine the flour, baking soda, and salt, then add this to the batter. Blend in the warm water. Add the bran and buttermilk and mix to incorporate.

4. Pour the batter into a well-greased muffin tin and bake for 20 minutes or until done.

Apple-Cheese Muffins

Makes 1½ dozen

1¾ cups all-purpose flour
1 teaspoon baking soda
1 teaspoon baking powder
½ teaspoon salt
3½ teaspoons ground cinnamon
¼ teaspoon ground cardamom
½ cup butter
1 cup granulated sugar
2 large eggs
¼ teaspoon almond extract
1 can (21 ounces) sliced apples, drained
1 cup shredded sharp cheddar cheese
¼ cup coffee

1. Preheat the oven to 375 degrees.

2. In a bowl, mix together the flour, soda, baking powder, salt, ½ teaspoon cinnamon, cardamom, and set aside.

3. In a large bowl, cream together the butter and ½ cup sugar. Beat in the eggs, one at a time, and blend well. Add the dry ingredients and the almond extract.

4. Reserve 18 slices of apple and chop the remaining ones. Add them to the batter, along with the cheese and coffee.

5. Fill the well-greased cups of a muffin tin one-quarter full with the batter.

6. Combine the remaining sugar and the cinnamon. Sprinkle this mixture over the 18 apple slices, then press 1 sugared apple slice into each muffin cup. Cover with the remaining batter until cups are two-thirds full.

7. Bake the muffins about 20 minutes, or until done. Remove from the tin and cool on a wire rack.

Date-Nut Muffins   Makes 3 dozen

2 cups soy flour
1 cup powdered milk
1 teaspoon salt
1 tablespoon baking powder
1 cup chopped dates
1 cup chopped nuts
3 large eggs, lightly beaten
3 tablespoons butter, melted
2 teaspoons grated orange rind
¾ cup orange juice
3 tablespoons honey

1. Preheat the oven to 350 degrees.

2. In a bowl, combine the flour, milk powder, salt, and baking powder. Add the dates and nuts, mixing to coat them with the dry mixture.

3. In another bowl, combine the remaining ingredients, then stir in the dry mixture.

4. Pour the batter into a well-greased muffin tin and bake for 25 minutes, or until done.

Sweet Potato Muffins   Makes 2 dozen

1½ cups granulated sugar
1¼ cups cooked, mashed sweet potatoes or yams
½ cup butter
2 large eggs
1 cup milk
1½ cups all-purpose flour
2 teaspoons baking powder
1¼ teaspoons cinnamon
¼ teaspoon ground nutmeg
¼ teaspoon salt
½ cup raisins
¼ cup chopped walnuts or pecans

1. Preheat the oven to 400 degrees.

2. In a bowl, combine 1¼ cups sugar, the potatoes, and the butter. Mix until smooth, then add the eggs and milk, and mix.

3. In another bowl, mix together the flour, baking powder, 1 teaspoon cinnamon, nutmeg, and salt. Add the dry mixture to the batter, stirring just until blended.

4. Fold in the raisins and nuts, then spoon the batter into a well-greased muffin tin.

5. Combine the remaining sugar and cinnamon and sprinkle it over the batter. Bake for 25 to 30 minutes, or until done.

SWEET BREADS

Apple Bread   Makes 1 loaf

4 tablespoons grated
  sharp cheddar cheese
⅔ cup apple juice
3 tablespoons butter, melted
¾ cup brown sugar
1 large egg, lightly beaten
2 cups all-purpose flour
½ small apple, peeled, cored, and thinly sliced

1½ teaspoons baking soda
1 teaspoon baking powder
½ teaspoon salt
½ teaspoon ground cinnamon
¼ teaspoon ground nutmeg
½ cup peeled and grated apple

1. Preheat the oven to 325 degrees.

2. Generously grease a 9 × 5-inch loaf pan. On the bottom and sides of the pan, sprinkle as much of the grated cheese as will stick; reserve the remainder.

3. In a mixing bowl, combine the apple juice, butter, brown sugar, and egg.

4. In another bowl, sift together the flour, baking soda, baking powder, salt, and spices, then add it to the juice mixture.

5. Add the grated apples and stir to blend. Lightly pour the batter into the loaf pan. Sprinkle the remainder of the cheese over it and arrange the apple slices in a pattern across the top of the loaf.

6. Bake the loaf for 50 minutes, or until done. Don't overcook the loaf; the bread should be just golden.

Banana Bread   Makes 1 loaf

½ cup butter
1 cup brown sugar
2 large eggs
1 cup mashed bananas
¾ cup crunchy peanut butter

1 cup whole-wheat flour
1 cup all-purpose flour
½ teaspoon salt
½ teaspoon baking soda

1. In a mixing bowl, cream together the butter and sugar. Add the eggs, and mix well.

2. Stir in the bananas and the peanut butter and blend thoroughly.

3. In another bowl, combine the dry ingredients and then add to the creamed mixture. Pour the batter into a well-greased loaf pan. Let the batter stand at room temperature for 20 minutes.

4. Preheat the oven to 350 degrees.

5. Bake the loaf for 45 minutes to 1 hour, or until done.

COOKIES

Carob Chip Cookies   Makes 3 dozen

½ cup butter
¾ cup brown sugar
2 large eggs, lightly beaten
2 teaspoons vanilla extract
¾ cup whole-wheat pastry flour
¼ cup all-purpose flour

⅓ cup wheat germ
½ cup powdered milk
2 teaspoons baking powder
½ teaspoon salt
1 package (6 ounces) carob chips
½ cup chopped nuts

1. Preheat the oven to 375 degrees.

2. In a large bowl, cream together the butter and the sugar. Beat in the eggs and add the vanilla.

3. In another bowl, sift together the flours, wheat germ, milk powder, baking powder, and salt. Add the dry mixture to the batter.

4. Stir in the carob chips and nuts. Drop by teaspoonfuls onto a greased baking sheet and bake until cookies are light brown — about 8 to 10 minutes.

Peanut Butter-Bran Cookies — Makes 7½ dozen

1 cup butter
½ cup peanut butter
1 cup brown sugar
1 cup granulated sugar
1 teaspoon vanilla extract
2 large eggs

1 teaspoon baking soda
1½ cups all-purpose flour
1 cup quick-cooking oats
2 cups raisin bran cereal
1 teaspoon ground cinnamon
1 cup chopped pecans

1. Preheat the oven to 350 degrees.

2. In a mixing bowl, cream together the butter, peanut butter, brown sugar, and white sugar. Mixture should be light and fluffy. Add the vanilla and the eggs, and beat until smooth.

3. Add the remaining ingredients and mix well. Drop the batter by teaspoonfuls onto an ungreased baking sheet and bake about 10 minutes. The cookies will puff, then fall. Remove them from the sheet and cool on wire racks.

Three-Fruit Bars   16 two-inch squares

1½ cups whole-wheat pastry flour
⅓ cup wheat germ
2 teaspoons baking powder
½ teaspoon salt
1½ cups combined chopped dates, prunes, and apricots
½ cup chopped walnuts
3 tablespoons sesame seeds
3 large eggs
½ cup vegetable oil
½ cup honey
1 teaspoon vanilla extract

1. Preheat the oven to 325 degrees.

2. In a mixing bowl, combine the flour, wheat germ, baking powder, and salt. Stir in the fruit, nuts, and seeds and mix to coat with the dry mixture.

3. In another bowl, combine the eggs with the oil, honey, and vanilla. Add the dry ingredients, stirring lightly. Spread the mixture in a greased 8-inch-square baking dish.

4. Bake until done — about 35 to 40 minutes. Cool before cutting into squares.

Whole-Wheat—Oatmeal Raisin Bars

Makes 7 dozen

¾ cup butter
⅔ cup honey
2 large eggs
2 teaspoons vanilla extract
2½ cups rolled oats
1 cup whole-wheat pastry flour
2 teaspoons baking powder
½ teaspoon salt
½ cup chopped nuts
½ cup raisins

1. Preheat the oven to 325 degrees.

2. In a mixing bowl, cream together the butter and honey. Add the eggs and the vanilla and mix well.

3. In another bowl, combine the oats, flour, baking powder, and salt. Add the nuts and raisins and stir to coat with the dry mixture.

4. Add the dry mixture to the batter and stir to blend. Spread the batter in a lightly greased 11 × 7-inch baking pan and bake for 25 to 30 minutes. Cool before cutting into squares.

Bran-Apricot Bars   Makes 2 dozen

½ cup diced dried apricots   2 large eggs
1 cup boiling water   1 cup brown sugar
½ cup butter   ½ teaspoon vanilla extract
¼ cup granulated sugar   ½ teaspoon baking powder
1 cup all-purpose flour   ½ teaspoon salt
¾ cup bran buds   ½ cup chopped walnuts

1. Preheat the oven to 350 degrees.

2. Combine the apricots with the water in a pot and simmer 10 minutes. Drain and set the apricots aside.

3. In a large mixing bowl, cream the butter and sugar until fluffy. Stir in ½ cup flour and the bran buds. Press this mixture into the bottom of a 9 × 9 × 2-inch baking pan. Bake for 15 minutes, then remove from the oven.

4. Meanwhile, beat the eggs until thick and lemon colored. Add the remaining ingredients except the walnuts and apricots. Mix well, then stir in the apricots and walnuts.

5. Pour the mixture into the baked crust. Return to the oven for 25 to 30 minutes. Cool before cutting into 2 × 1-inch bars.

Wheat Germ-Cheese Bars   Makes 16 2-inch bars

½ pound sharp cheddar cheese, finely grated
1 cup whole-wheat flour
¼ cup wheat germ
½ teaspoon baking powder
¼ teaspoon salt
⅛ teaspoon cayenne pepper
3 tablespoons vegetable oil
¼ cup milk
⅓ cup finely chopped nuts

1. Preheat the oven to 350 degrees.

2. In a mixing bowl, combine the cheese with the flour, coating the cheese to prevent lumping. Add the wheat germ, baking powder, salt, and pepper and mix well.

3. Add the remaining ingredients. Press the mixture into a greased 8-inch-square baking dish, and bake for 20 to 25 minutes, or until done. Cool before cutting into squares.

RECOMMENDED READING

Ewald, Ellen B. *Recipes for a Small Planet.* New York: Ballantine, 1975.

Lappé, Frances M. *Diet for a Small Planet.* New York: Ballantine, 1975.

Moore, Kathleen, ed. *Vegetarian Time's Guide to Dining in the U.S.A.* New York: Atheneum, 1979.

Null, Gary, and Null, Steve. *The New Vegetarian.* New York: Dell, 1975.

Roberts, Richard, and Riker, Tom. *The Directory of Health and Natural Foods: A Sourcebook for a Dietary Revolution.* New York: G.P. Putnam, 1979.

Thomas, Anna. *The Vegetarian Epicure.* New York: Knopf, 1972.

INDEX

A Alfalfa Sprouts, 185–86
Amino acids, 11–13
Anchovy butter, 54
Appetizers, 119, 163, 199, 200–1, 223, 224, 225, 226, 227
Apple(s): Bread, 308; Cheese Muffins, 304–5; Chutney, 256; Milk, 285; Peanut Butter Dessert, 249; Roquefort and Apple Omelette, 198; Snack, 278
Apricot Whip, 246
Aromatic Salt, 47
Asparagus, 106–9

B Banana(s): Bread, 309; Curried with Yogurt, 247; Delight, 247
Barbecue Sauce, 68
Barley, 89–91. *Also* Bean with Barley Soup, 167; with Butter and cheese, 98; Salad, 97; Vegetable Stew, 95; Yogurt and Barley Soup, 218
Basic Loaf, 291–92
Batter-Fried Asparagus, 108–9
Beans, dried, 160–82
Bean sprouts, 184–94
Bean with Barley Soup, 167
Beets, 110–12
Best Biscuits Yet, 298
Biscuits, 298–300
Black bean(s): Bisque with Sherry, 162–63; Lasagne, 168; with Rice, 166–67; Soup with Rice, 164–65
Black French Dressing, 65
Blueberry Cream, 248
Blue Cheese Dressing, 66
Borani, 147

Bourbon-Baked Beans, 182
Bourbon Delight, 62
Bran: Apricot Bars, 314; Muffins, 303
Brandied Vinegar, 59
Bread(s), 291–97, 308–9
Broccoli, 112–14. *Also* Pasta with Broccoli, 207
Brown rice: Burgers, 80; and Carrot Soup, 79; Mexican, 81; Mushroom-Rice Casserole, 82; Sesame Tomatoes on Rice, 88
Buckwheat, 89
Bulgur: Lentil and Bulgur Pilaf, 176; Rice Pilaf with, 85; Seed Loaf, 92; Tabbouleh, 96
Butter, Mock, 57
Buttermilk, Pink, 287
Butters, flavored, 52–54

C Café au Chocolat, 285
Cabbage, 115–16
Calcium, 14–15
Caponata, 119
Carob: Chip Cookies, 310; Fluff, 249; Syrup, 256
Carrot(s), 117. *Also* Brown Rice Soup, 79
Caviar, 223–225
Celery, 118
Cheddar Butter, 53
Cheese, 199–205. *Also* Apple-Cheese Muffins, 304–5; -Baked Celery, 118; Baked Eggs with, 197; Bread, 297; Cottage Cheese Delight, 261; Crab in Cheese Pastries, 236–37; Eggplant Purée, 120; Fried Spinach with, 139; Garden Sandwich, 262; Grilled Mushrooms and, 263; Grilled Tuna with, 264; Hot Clam-Cheese Dip, 226; Pasta with Roquefort, 210; Pears with Roquefort, 210; Roquefort and Apple Omelette, 198; Shrimp

in a Cheese Ring, 234–35; Tofu-Cheese Rarebit, 193; Wheat Germ-Cheese Bars, 315; Yogurt Sauce, 73
Cheesies, 274
Chili Beans, Baked, 172
Chili Powder, 50
Chili Sandwich, Open-Faced, 264
Chinese Broth, 75
Chinese Hot Mustard Sauce, 71
Chinese Style Asparagus, 106
Chutney: Apple, 256; Nut-Wich, 261
Clam(s): -Cheese Dip, Hot, 226; Quiche in Wheat-Germ Pastry, 238–39; -Zucchini Soup, 228
Coffee Ice Cream Supreme, 254
Conserie D'Harissa, 50
Cookies, 310–15
Corn. See Hominy Grits
Corn Muffins, 301
Cottage Cheese Delight, 261
Couscous: Basic, 102–3; Sweet, 104
Crab: in Cheese Pastries, 236–37; Wontons, 233
Cream Cheese, Mock, 55
Cucumber(s): and Beets in Cream, 110; Caviar, 223; Soup, Chilled, 216
Curried Cashews, 270
Curry Marinade, 62–63
Curry Powder, 48

D Daiquiri, Frozen, 286
Date-Nut Muffins, 306
Dill Marinade, 63

E Egg(s), 197–98. Also Hominy Grits with, 99; and Mushroom Patties, 131; Sprouts with Spiced, 188–89; Tofu and Bean Sprout Omelette, 194

Egg Noodles with Walnut Sauce, 206
Eggplant, 119–21. Also Broiled Sandwich, 265
Egyptian Michoteta, 205

F Felafel with Tahini Sauce, 170–71
Fettuccine: with Green Beans, 208; with Zucchini and Mushrooms, 209
Fish, 243–44
Food additives, 34–35, 37–39
Fruit: desserts, 246–52. Also Apple Chutney, 256; Fruit Syrup, 255; Spirited Fruit, 255

G Garden Sandwich, 262
Garlic Butter, 53
Gingered Yogurt, 251
Gnocchi, 138
Golden Bowties, 275
Granola: basic recipe, 281; My Granola, 282
Green beans, 122–23. Also with Fettuccini, 208
Greek Lentil Soup, 165
Green Crab Soup, 229

H Harissa Sauce, 70
Herb Butter, 53
Herbed Cocktail Biscuits, 299
High Fiber Slaw, 102
Hominy grits, 99–100
Hot Slaw, 115

I Iron, 15
Italian Dressing, 66–67
Italian Seasoning, 48–49

K Kasha: Balls, 94; Basic, 93
Kidney Beans in Red Wine, 171
Kusherie, 181

L Lemon: Butter, 54; Pepper, 49; Yogurt Sauce, 74
  Lentil(s): and Bulgur Pilaf, 176; Burgers, 179; Curried, 173; -Nut Loaf, 180; and Spinach Pilaf, 177; and Spinach Squares, 178
  Lima Bean Soup, 124
  Lime Butter, 54

M Marinades, 62–65
  Marmalade, Spirited, 257
  Mayonnaise: Tofu, 58; Yogurt, 58
  Meatless (Vegetable) Loaf, 155
  Menu-planning hints, 20
  Mexican Brown Rice, 81
  Middle Eastern Spice, 47
  Mint Vinegar, 60
  Minted Peas, 135
  Miso, 190. *Also* Dressing and Marinade, 64–65
  Muffins, 301–7
  Mujaddarah, 174
  Mung Bean Sprouts, 186. *See also* Bean Sprouts
  Mushroom(s), 125–31. *Also* Barley Soup, 90; Caviar, 224; and Cheese, Grilled, 263; Cheese and Mushroom Balls, 200; Fettuccine with Zucchini and, 209; Potatoes Stuffed with, 137; Rice Casserole, 82; Roquefort, 201–2; Sautéed Tofu and, 192–3
  Mustard Butter, 53

N Nachos Sandwich, 266
  Natural foods, descriptions of, 21–32
  North African Rice with Spinach and Lentils, 175
  Nut Balls, 279
  Nutty Onions, 134
  Nutty Wild Rice Ring, 83

O Onion(s), 132–34. *Also* Miso Soup with Onions and Spinach, 190; Soup, Chilled, 284; Whole-Wheat Onion Biscuits, 300
  Orange: Shake, 286; Sherbet, 253
  Oyster and Spinach Soup, 230

P Parmesan Crowns, 201
  Parsley Butter, 52
  Pasta, 206–12
  Peanut Butter: Apple, 249; Balls, 279; -Bran Cookies, 311; Dressing, 67; Sandwich, Crunchy, 262
  Peanut Sauce, 71
  Pears with Roquefort, 248
  Peas, 135
  Peppers, 136
  Pesticides, 36–37
  Pesto Sauce, 70
  Pilaf (Rice), 84
  Pita (Pocket) Bread, 296–97
  Pocket Sandwich, 268
  Potato(es), 137–38. *Also* -Asparagus Salad, 107; Chips, 276; Caviar Potatoes, 225; Peel Crisps, 277
  Preheated Oil, 51
  Prunes, Poached in Wine, 250

R Riboflavin, 14
  Rice, 78–88. *Also* Black Beans with, 166–67; Black Bean Soup with, 164–65; Broccoli and Rice Casserole, 114; North African Rice with Spinach and Lentils, 175; Scallop and Lemon Rice Salad, 239. *See also* Brown Rice
  Roasted Peppers, 136
  Roasted Sunflower Seeds, 273
  Roquefort: and Apple Omelette, 198; Mushrooms, 201

Rye and Walnut Bread, 294

S Salad: Dressing(s), 64–67; Herbs, 49
Salads, 86–87, 97, 102, 107, 110, 148, 189, 211, 212, 239
Salmon: Bisque, 243; Loaf, 244
Sauces, 68–74
Scallops: Broiled, 231; and Lemon Rice Salad, 239
Sesame: Seed Fingers, 280; Tomatoes on Rice, 88
Shellfish, 226–37
Shrimp: Dip, 227; in a Cheese Ring, 234–35; Scampi, 232
Soups, 79, 90, 112, 116, 124, 125, 128, 132–33, 140, 162–63, 164–65, 167, 190, 202, 216, 217, 218, 228, 229, 230, 242, 243, 284
Sour Cream, Mock, 55–56
Soy Nuts, 272
Soy Sauce, Spicy, 72
Spaghetti Sauce, 68–69
Spices, 46–50
Spinach, 139–48. *Also* Lentil and Spinach Pilaf, 177; Lentil and Spinach Squares, 178; Miso Soup with Onions and, 190; North African Rice with Spinach and Lentils, 175; Oyster and Spinach Soup, 230
Sprouts with Spiced Eggs, 188–89. *See also* Bean Sprouts
Stocks, 75–76
Strawberries: Carob-Dipped, 251; Orange, 252
Summertime Soup, 284
Sweet-and-Sour: Red Cabbage, 116; Sauce, 72–73; Sprouts, 187
Sweet Potato Muffins, 307

T Tabbouleh, 96, 268

Tamale Bean Pie, 169
Tempeh, Basic Fried, 191–92
Three-Fruit: Bars, 312; Drink, 288
Tiger's Milk Shake, 287
Toasted Pecans or Mixed Nuts, 271
Tofu, 192–94. *Also* Mayonnaise, 58
Tomato(es), 149–50. *Also* Creamy Cocktail, 283; Sauce Uncooked, 69; Sesame Tomatoes on Rice, 88; -Yogurt, Chilled, 217
Tuna with Cheese, Grilled, 264

V Vegetable(s), 106–57. *Also* Barley Stew, 95; in a Shell, 156–57; Stock, 76; -Topped Tortillas, 267
Vegetarianism, health benefits of, 10–11; risks, 11, 13, 16
Vinegars, 59–61
Virgin Mary, 283
Vitamin B$_{12}$, 13–14
Vitamin D, 15–16

W Wheat Germ: -Bran Bread, 292–93; -Cheese Bars, 315
Whole-Wheat: -Oatmeal Raisin Bars, 313; -Onion Biscuits, 300
Wild Rice: Ring, 83; Salad, 86–87
Wine Vinegar, 61

Y Yogurt, 213–20. *Also* Cheese Sauce, 73; Curried Bananas with, 247; Gingered, 251; Lemon Sauce, 74; Mayonnaise, 58; Mint Marinade, 64; -Wheat-Germ Muffins, 302

Z Zinc, 15
Zucchini, 151–54. *Also* Clam-Zucchini Soup, 228; Fettuccine with Zucchini and Mushrooms, 209